QUANTUM

DOWSING FOR HEALTH

The Applications & Methods For Holistic Healing

Arthur Bailey

1991
Llewellyn Publications
St. Paul, Minnesota 55164-0383, U.S.A.

Q quantum © W. Foulsham & Co. Ltd.

First U.S. Edition, 1991
First Printing, 1991

Cover art by Tom Canny

Library of Congress Cataloging-in-Publication Data
  Bailey, Arthur, MSc.
    Dowsing for health: the applications & methods for holistic
  healing / Arthur Bailey.
        p.   cm.
    Includes bibliographical references and index.
    ISBN 0-87542-059-1
    1. Divining rod. 2. Alternative medicine. I. Title.
  BF1628.B24   1991   90-24279
  133.3′ 23—dc20   CIP

This Llewellyn/Quantum edition produced for
U.S.A. and Canada under license by:

Llewellyn Publications
A Division of Llewellyn Worldwide, Ltd.
P.O. Box 64383, St. Paul, MN 55164-0383, U.S.A.

CONTENTS

PREFACE

This book is based on my own experiences of dowsing and healing gained over twenty years. My background is that of an engineering scientist who became involved in dowsing by accident. Having proved to myself that dowsing did indeed work, I then did my utmost to find a rational explanation for the phenomenon. I have to admit that I failed to find an acceptable theory, dowsing being far wider in its possibilities and uses than can be explained on the basis of current scientific theory. Nevertheless, my investigations into dowsing led into what was for me a new area, that of healing and health. I discovered dowsing could be of immense help in obtaining information that was not otherwise known.

Throughout my searches I have tried to remain true to the spirit of scientific research. This is therefore a book about what I have discovered for myself, as I was not prepared to accept the opinions of others unless I had tested them out personally. This was essential as I discovered that dowsing was full of pseudo-scientific theories and over-complex methods of working, and I had to sort out the wheat from the chaff.

I define healing as bringing the mind and body to as complete a state of wholeness and ease as is possible for a person at a particular time. Just what is achievable for any one person will depend on many factors, not the least of which is the attitude of the person requiring help. I view healing as guiding and helping another, not just doing things to them.

The emphasis throughout this book is on encouraging you to try things out for yourself, and to put aside any doubts that you may have about your abilities. Dowsing is not a gift given to just a few, as some people have asserted in the past; rather it is an innate ability present in everyone. Dowsing can be a difficult concept to encompass, the idea that one can obtain information with the aid of a pendulum or pair of bent wires is not the easiest thing to accept.

The book starts with an introduction showing how my own dowsing began, how I reluctantly proceeded to go further and further into it, and finally how I arrived at the healing aspects of dowsing. This is followed by a brief history of dowsing, which is important in giving a firm background from which modern dowsing can be evaluated.

Next the basics of dowsing are covered, how to start, the pitfalls to avoid and how to keep things simple. There is no need whatever for some of the weird and complex ways of working that some people extol.

Then the practical health aspects of dowsing are examined, particularly diet and how this can affect one's health. From this point the book expands into dowsing for vitamins and other supplements.

The later chapters cover such diverse aspects as the bio-chemic remedies, flower remedies, homoeopathy, radionics and geopathic stress. The final chapters cover a wide range of healing techniques in which I have been privileged to work, including the use of spinal manipulation.

The intention throughout is to give an insight into what lies behind dowsing and its application to health, rather than just give a series of 'do this — do that' set of exercises. Safety lies in simplicity and having an open mind, and my approach is to 'de-mystify' dowsing as far as possible, for I can see no virtue whatever in using over-complicated methods and theories that just do not hold water. I therefore accept that some of the things that I say may well upset some people, and for this I make no apologies, as this is what is really meant by scientific objectivity: speaking the truth as you find it without fear or favour.

The text contains many examples taken from my own experience. It is hoped that these will not only illustrate the subject matter but also give support and encouragement to you to try things out for yourself. It is one thing reading about things, something quite different to take your courage in both hands and experience it for yourself, even though dowsing is more accepted now than when I started using it in the mid 1960s.

For me dowsing has become an invaluable tool, particularly in the realms of health and healing. In careful hands it can increase enormously your ability to improve your own health and that of others. My own life would have been immeasurably poorer, if one February I had not contracted a very bad dose of the 'flu . . .

Arthur Bailey

CHAPTER 1

THE RING OF TRUTH

The author's personal account of how he became interested in dowsing was through experiencing its remarkable effectiveness, from locating buried pipes and water to its applications in health and healing. Everything the author writes about is based on personal experience.

It all started with Asian Flu. Until that time I had been an orthodox engineering scientist teaching electronics at Bradford University. I had only a mild sceptical interest in occult matters. Nothing was further from my mind than getting involved with fringe subjects like dowsing.

Then the 'flu struck. I had only once before been so ill, a long time previously. I had no energy, even when the virus had departed. It was diagnosed by my doctor as Post-influenzal Syndrome, the modern term for this now being Myalgesic Encephalomyelitis (ME). A pharmacist friend of mine told me that this meant that they didn't really know why I was still ill: I should be better but I wasn't. I felt terrible, and the least exertion put me back in bed. So I watched evening television (this was before all-day television) and read books. I became desperate for things to read and finished up reading all sorts of things that previously I would have rejected. It was one of these books that started things off.

My mother lent a book to me by Beverley Nichols called *A Thatched Roof*[1]. It was largely autobiographical and in it he

---

1. Nichols, Beverley, *A Thatched Roof*, Jonathan Cape, 1933.

mentioned how a water diviner had found a much better water supply for his cottage. It sounded far-fetched, but yet it had a strange ring of truth. So I arranged for the local library to see if they had a book on dowsing — the name mentioned in the book for water divining. One was obtained for me from Halifax library and it did nothing to give me confidence. It was a translation from a French book. In it there were pictures of bearded Frenchmen in tall stove-pipe hats, and one picture I can still remember well; it was of a tall bearded man holding a pendulum in one hand and a tall cylinder labelled 'L'EAU' in the other. It all looked rather eccentric to say the least.

The book did however have a do-it-yourself section at the end. It mentioned the use of the pendulum, but also recommended the use of angle-rods for beginners. In this case they suggested two L-shaped pieces of fencing wire dropped into garden-cane bamboo handles (see Fig. 1).

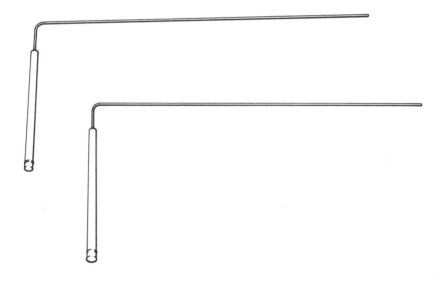

Figure 1. Angle-rods showing bamboo holders

I had problems with getting the rods to move freely until I discovered that it was important that the bottom of the handles were cut just below a 'node' in the stem. That way, when the wires are dropped into the handles they pivot on the solid bit of bamboo at the bottom. This can be seen from the photograph, where the wire that fits into the bamboo holder is longer than the holder that it drops into.

The handles were held vertically with the wires pointing in front and parallel (see Fig. 2). According to the book, walking over nearly any underground phenomenon, not just water, would make the rods move. Sceptically I made up a set of rods and tried walking slowly round the house. I felt very, very foolish! It was difficult to prevent moving the rods accidentally and the last breath of wind tended to move them. However, I persevered. Much to my surprise I found that the rods actually did move inwards over the gas-pipe, where it ran into the house. They also moved where the drains were but I was not convinced. Agreed, the rods had moved but I knew where those things were, and I knew sufficient about auto-suggestion to realise that I could unconsciously be making the rods move by reaction to my thoughts. Nothing had yet been proven at all, so far as I was concerned.

I started dowsing further afield, and to my surprise the rods kept moving together at certain points in the garden. There was nothing to be seen at these places, so I started putting down half-bricks as markers. There appeared to be no real pattern until I saw that about ten of these bricks made a straight line. This cut diagonally from the house corner out towards the front gate. Incredulous but excited I checked it all out, and there was no doubt about it. Every time I crossed that imaginary line that ran between the bricks, the rods moved. The water and electricity supplies both came into the house at that corner — could it be either of them? I checked the other side of the wall where my 'line' stopped. I picked it up at once. It ran straight out into the road and stopped about three quarters of the way across.

10

Figure 2. Angle-rods in use in the searching position

There was nothing to be seen where it ended. I rechecked it all and got the same result. I marked the end of my line and went in to think.

I had never found the cold water stop-tap outside the house. I knew where it should be as I had a set of the house plans, obtained from the original architect of the house. The plans showed the stop-tap to be about fifteen metres away from where my line ended. I had previously looked where the plans showed it to be, worried in case we got a burst on the mains side of the house stop-tap, and had found nothing. Could the plans be wrong? I went out with a large hammer and thumped the road surface where my line ended. It sounded just the same there as on the surrounding road. Finally I plucked up courage: I asked my wife to keep a sharp eye open for cars and official-looking people, and proceeded to chisel into the road (not to be recommended!). Two centimetres down I hit the stop-tap cover which had been tarred over for years.

I don't know who was the most shaken, myself or my wife. I had never expected it to work, had no idea of where the stop tap was, and had found it by dowsing. The odds of finding it by chance were extremely remote — they must have been thousands if not millions to one against. Auto-suggestion would have had me looking much further down the road. This can be seen from the map of the garden shown in Figure 3.

It was from this point in time that I delved further into dowsing. I suspected that it was magnetic in origin, and hoped to make a name for myself as the first person to explain this age-old phenomenon. I went on to do further dowsing and found that it really did work. It found things for me that I never knew were there, and it worked time and time again. I must emphasise though that I have always kept a critical approach to my investigations, as it is all too easy to get carried away by one's own beliefs and enthusiasms.

I have always tried to maintain my scientific objectivity, no matter what the subject. The true scientist knows that it is the experiment that matters, not the theory. Theories are there to try to achieve a common understanding from what otherwise are disconnected events. If experimental results cannot be explained by current theories, then it may well be that those theories are too limited.

12

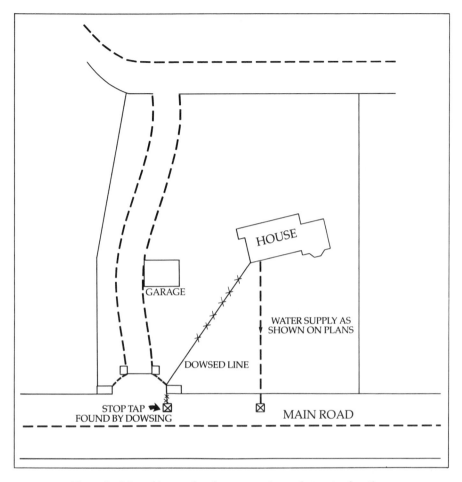

Figure 3. Map of house showing water pipe and stop tap locations

In certain circles, experimental results that do not fit the theories must, virtually by definition, be incorrect. Nothing must challenge the established theories, because those theories are 'true'. Bigotry exists just as much in science as in religion.

I well remember giving a lecture at one annual congress of the British Society of Dowsers. I was talking on the medical applications of dowsing, and afterwards I was accosted by a rather upset medical practitioner. He asked me how on earth someone with my obviously impeccable scientific qualifications was concerning myself with such quackery. I told him that my experience was that it worked, as I had said in my talk. He persisted. He was obviously upset and challenged me to prove to him that dowsing worked. Now this is a trap that the unwary can easily fall into: in trying to prove the validity of dowsing, you finish up working to the rules set by the other person, rather than working as you usually do. I refused to bite. I said, truthfully, that it would take far too long to talk about it. I suggested that if he was really interested in the validity of dowsing, then he should read a really good book on the subject. I personally could recommend such a book to him. He could then try it out for himself and see how he got on, and if he found no adequate results, then I would be only too happy to talk to him about it.

'I haven't time to waste on such nonsense!' he exclaimed, and left me.

I have learned by bitter experience that it is just no use trying to convince anyone who has fixed ideas to the contrary, on any subject; let alone dowsing. It is just a waste of effort. Such people are not interested in what you are saying, all they are doing is looking for the least flaw in what you are putting to them. Once they find any fault, however small, that is then used to justify why you are deluded and they are right.

Everything that I am writing about in this book is from my own experience. I have been dowsing for over twenty-two years now, and have covered a wide field within that time. One thing is certain, there are many facets of life that cannot be explained by current orthodox scientific theories. This may be uncomfortable to some, but I know from my own experience that it is true.

Scientific breakthroughs have largely been made by those willing to buck the system, otherwise one stays only in safe known areas. Just because a scientist says that dowsing, or clairvoyance or something else, has no validity, it means nothing. It is normally just their opinion based on totally inadequate theories. One only has to look at the history of science to find that, like all other histories, it is littered with mistaken ideas and beliefs. Poor Galileo suffered terribly for suggesting ideas that were not in accordance with the current dogma of the day. If we believe that modern science is now quite different, with scientists purely dedicated to the Truth, then we are making a serious error. The basic problem is that of human nature, the desire for security and approval of one's peers. It needs a very determined hardy soul to go out on a limb and risk total opposition to his or her ideas and work.

This book is not intended as a Do-It-Yourself guide to dowsing. Such books already exist and are mentioned in the footnotes. It is a guide to the many applications that dowsing has in the fields of health and healing. The main thing is to have a go yourself. It takes time to become competent, as in acquiring any skill, but it will reveal many things of great benefit. It does work, that I can assure you, but only you can prove it to your own satisfaction.

There are many well-documented cases showing where water diviners have succeeded, against all the predictions of geologists, in finding water. One of the best documented cases was when a dowser found a large underground reservoir completely unknown in the local geological survey and a whole series of test drillings were taken to prove his findings[2]. His dowsing resulted in saving the British Forces in Germany a large expenditure on new water-treatment plants. One must always remember, however, that no amount of careful well-documented work will convince the complete sceptic, who says it must be due to 'local knowledge' or 'coincidence' or 'seeing visual clues'.

If you are sceptical, but still have an open mind, fine. Have a go and see how you get on. Like me, you might very well surprise yourself.

---

2. Grattan, Colonel H., CBE, 'A Successful Feat', *Practical Dowsing*, pp. 62–77, G. Bell and Sons Ltd., 1965.

CHAPTER 2
STRANGER THAN FICTION

Dowsing is not a recent discovery but has a long history. The earliest recorded uses were in locating metallic ores. Scientific investigations were carried out for the first time in the early part of this century, and since that time much work has been done, including investigations into the brain rhythms of dowsers.

The origins of dowsing are lost in pre-history. There is an Egyptian mural showing someone holding a forked rod, but it is not certain what the person was doing. Some people have supposed that it was a dowser looking for gold, but such ideas are pure conjecture. The earliest definite reference to a divining rod was in about 1430, where the rod was used for locating metallic ores[3]. This reference is very brief; it only mentions the use of a divining rod, not how it was used. The next reference was by Martin Luther in 1518, when he declared that the use of a divining rod broke the first commandment. Incidentally, there are still some people who, to this day, insist that dowsing originates from the devil. For justification they usually quote the book of Deuteronomy as a biblical reference, classing dowsing as being the same thing as soothsaying and divining from animal entrails. Just for the record, it may be noticed that the same people never quote the following part of the scripture which gives the Jewish people the right to subjugate other races on the earth.

---

3. Solea, Andreas de, *Eröffnulte und blosgestellte Natur*, details given in Keiserwetter, C., *Gesichte des Neueren Occultimus*, 1891–95, i. 512, ii. 382.

In 1530, G. Agricola published a short essay where dowsing was mentioned as being used as a help in mining[4], this being followed in 1556 by his long work called *De Re Metallica*. This book is perhaps best known for its woodcut illustrations, which are often shown in contemporary books on dowsing. The most famous one (see Fig. 4) shows all the stages in dowsing from cutting a branch from a tree, holding the rod, the rod dipping, to ore being excavated. Agricola pointed out that the rod cannot move in response to a force exerted on it by the minerals underground because the rod will not work for everyone, a point overlooked by some people, even today. The earliest known illustration of a dowser at work appears in a book called *Cosmographica Universalis* by S. Munster that was published in 1550. Unfortunately there is no mention made in the text that refers to the illustration.

The first British reference to dowsing was in 1639 by Gabriel Plattes[5], who mentions how to cut rods and use them for the location of metallic ores. This was followed by an increasing number of articles on divining and the divining rod.

By 1710, the use of divining techniques must have been known widely, as Jonathan Swift published the following satirical verse:

> They tell us something strange and odd,
> About a certain Magick Rod,
> That, bending down its Top, divines
> When e'er the Soil has Golden Mines:
> Where there are none, it stands erect,
> Scorning to show the least Respect.

---

4. Agricola, G., 'Bermannus', p. 135.

5. Plattes, G., *A Discovery of Subterreneall Treasure*, pp. 11–13.

Figure 4. Early mineral dowsers in action. From De Re Metallica, G. Agricola, 1556

In 1641, the Jesuit, Athanasius Kircher[6], made the discovery that the rod's movements were due to unconscious muscular action. Unfortunately this discovery was later largely forgotten by dowsers who reverted to the theory of an affinity between the rod and the element being sought.

From the end of the seventeenth century there were numerous books published on dowsing, including the use of the rod in finding water as well as mineral deposits. Equally there were many articles published against dowsing — the majority apparently being motivated by religious belief rather than objective evidence of fraud. It was only in the latter part of the eighteenth century that any detailed investigation of dowsing was undertaken and recorded. This was undertaken by a Dr Thouvenel who investigated three exceptional French dowsers, Parangue, Bleton and Pennet[7]. His results maintained French interest in both public and academic circles for over a quarter of a century. This is no doubt why dowsing continued to be more acceptable in France than Britain, even up to the present day. There were exceptional dowsers in Britain, John Mullins of the last century being one, but their activities never reached the public here in anything like the same way.

SCIENTIFIC INVESTIGATIONS

The first real scientific investigation into dowsing in the UK was carried out by Barrett and Besterman[8] in the early part of this century. Their book *The Divining Rod* is a readable

---

6.   Kircher, A., *Magnes* (1641), pp. 25–8; also *Mundus Subterraeneus* (1665), pp. 181–2.

7.   Thouvenel, Dr, *Memoire physique et medicinale* (1781); *Seconde memoire* (1784).

8.   Barrett, Sir William, and Besterman, Theodore, *The Divining Rod*, 1926; Republished 1968 by University Books Inc.

account of dowsing early this century. The investigations were carefully done, even taking British dowsers over to Ireland to dowse on a pre-selected site. The results of this latter investigation were conclusive. The dowsers, none of whom knew each other, gave nearly identical locations where water was to be found. The results were then verified by drilling where the dowsers had indicated and also drilling elsewhere on the site. The dowsers proved to be accurate in finding the water that was present on that site, the other bore-holes being virtually dry. In spite of this and countless other carefully controlled investigations, there are still people who claim that dowsing has been proven not to work. It may be worth noting at this point that setting up an experiment that does not give positive answers means just that — and no more. If conditions are incorrect then results may not occur. Barrett and Besterman tested dowsers in their working environments, not in an artificially set up laboratory. Pandas fail to reproduce under laboratory conditions, but that does not mean that pandas cannot breed.

Early this century the vast majority of water-finders in this country used the classical forked rod. Indeed the forked rod always tends to be associated with dowsers. It appears to have been the French dowsers who preferred to use the pendulum. Now a forked rod is difficult to hold correctly (see p. 33 for details); it has to be held 'spring-loaded'. It is this tension put into the rod that causes it to move in the hands of the dowser. Because of this difficulty in holding the rod correctly, it was therefore reputed that only a few gifted persons could become water-diviners. If one is going to keep competition away, then such folklore is very profitable! On the other hand the forked rod is a better outdoor tool than the pendulum, as it is not affected by strong winds.

It was the French dowsers that we have to thank for much of the origins of the healing applications of dowsing. Not only that, but much of the healing work originated from within the Catholic Church. This is really quite surprising considering that, as mentioned previously, many religions have been firmly against divining.

For healing applications, the pendulum has many advantages. It only requires one hand, leaving the other one free to point if necessary. It is not confined to simple up–down responses like the forked rod. It is also more sensitive: this can be both a blessing and a curse as we shall see later. It was the venturing into healing that really brought dowsing into areas of contention. Up to that point, it had been commonly believed that dowsing was a direct physical reaction, the discoveries of Kirchner regarding muscular response having being forgotten. It was suggested that it was the result of the body reacting to something given off by underground water or minerals. This 'effluvia' as it was originally called, affected sensitive people. Even today these ideas have currency, only now the effluvia is called electromagnetic radiation.

Even before healing appeared on the scene, there was increasing evidence that a simple explanation was not possible. Some old dowsers had discovered how they could save themselves a lot of leg work. They sent a boy out to walk over a field where water was being looked for. The dowser remained stationary at the side of the field, watching the boy, and holding his dowsing rod. When the boy walked over a place where there was underground water, the rod moved in the dowser's hands. This is sometimes called dowsing at second-hand or dowsing by proxy. This is not easy to explain. It cannot be a response to radiations being given off just in the vertical direction from water flows. So how is it that the dowser reacts to where the boy is? Problems, problems!

Even within orthodox water divining there were other puzzling features. These arose from a natural desire to know if the water would be pure, and how far down one needed to dig. The variety of techniques used for these purposes was wide and sometimes conflicting. For example, some dowsers, having found an underground water flow, would determine its depth by an 'equal distance' method. They would mark the centre of the water flow, and then walk away from the stream until the rod moved again. They would then mark this second place. The distance between the two points on the ground surface was then equal to the depth of the stream from the surface. This method is still widely used today[9]. But other dowsers would use exactly the same method to determine the flow rate! For example every foot distance from the centre of the stream could correspond with 100 gallons per hour of flow rate.

This split the dowsers into two broad camps. One group believed that dowsing was a direct physical effect on the dowser. The second group believed that it was all under the mental control of the dowser, who had some sort of mind-link with the material being sought. Many dowsers felt that it was perhaps a mixture of the two, depending on circumstances. This degree of confusion was ideal ammunition for the opponents of dowsing, some of whom made full use of it. Indeed, as recently as ten years ago there was still a large split between the beliefs of the dowsing fraternity. This was unfortunate but natural, as people have always wished to understand more of the universe around them, and it is this desire that creates theories. When conflicting theories arise, it is a lack of information that is the problem. Unfortunately it is also human nature to become involved with arguing which is the best theory, instead of settling down and exploring the whole matter more thoroughly. The purely physical explanation has long been quite untenable. The differing methods of 'depthing' are but one example.

Map dowsing is perhaps one of the most bizarre examples to the newcomer — but yet it works. I well remember first reading about map dowsing; I nearly dismissed the whole matter out of hand. Then I remembered that it was only some six months previously that I had nearly dismissed

9. Graves, Tom, *The Diviner's Handbook*, p. 27, The Aquarian Press, 1986.

dowsing the same way. By then I knew beyond any shadow of doubt that dowsing worked, so I tried, sceptically, some map-dowsing. First of all I tried it using a pendulum over a sketch map of our house and garden. (For how to use a pendulum see p. 38.) Much to my surprise the pendulum swung into circles over places where the drains and cold-water supply ran. There was no doubt about it, I was finding positive accurate results. However, this was no proof, as autosuggestion could so easily be making the pendulum move. I therefore had a chat with my next-door neighbour, Jack. I knew that he was somewhat sceptical of my dowsing activities, which he had watched from his house but nevertheless I felt he would help me. I told him of my interest in map-dowsing and in trying it out to see if it really worked. Jack therefore drew me a large plan of his house and garden in Nottingham where he used to live. It showed just the outline of his house and garage and two parallel roads, one at each side of the house, nothing else. He told me that if my dowsing worked I would find something strange about the cold-water supply to the house.

I started dowsing over the map, and wherever the pendulum swung into a circle I put a cross on the map. I went backwards and forwards over the map in a series of parallel movements, gradually working my way down the map. When I had finished I connected up all the points that seemed to be linked to each other, and if in doubt I checked between points to see if I still experienced a reaction.

Apparently I was quite correct in my dowsing. I had discovered a line that went diagonally from the pavement towards the house, then straightened up and went at right angles from the road into the house. This was the water supply that Jack had mentioned. He said that he knew it went that way because he had once been digging deeply in his rose bed and had unearthed the pipe just where it bent. I had dowsed the drains as going out to the other road, and the position of those too was correct. Once again I was pretty shaken, for such things had no right to happen. All the scientific theories that I had been putting forward, based on magnetism, fell to the ground, and I was again faced with the apparently impossible that had worked.

I did not accept that one experiment as proof — I went further to check and recheck. Finally I did a full 'double-blind' test. A colleague of mine, Tony, organised the test. He asked some members of a parent-teachers' group to send me sketch maps of their houses, but they were not to tell him if they had sent me one. Equally they were not to give any indication as to who had sent the map, nor was the house to be identifiable (no road names, etc.), so I did not know who sent me the maps to dowse, nor where the houses were, and no-one but the senders knew that they had sent me a map.

Two maps duly arrived. One later turned out to be a waste of time, as the person who sent it did not know what was underground. The second had been sent by a sceptical architect — or so he was until he saw the map when I had finished with it.

I presented my results at a parent-teachers' meeting where I was giving a talk on dowsing at the request of Tony. He noticed an incredulous-looking person sitting on the front row during the early part of my talk. This turned out to be the architect who had sent me one of the maps.

When I pinned up the map that he had sent and started talking about what I had found, his face was a picture; I was 100 per cent correct! I had correctly located the cold-water supply, the drains and two large stone soak-aways in his garden, which used to be an orchard. I also located an underground stream that he knew nothing about, but later found for himself by dowsing. Under such conditions any physical explanation based on current scientific theories is quite unacceptable.

Earlier this century, one of the outstanding French map dowsers was Abbé Mermet. He was an expert, and there were many many people who vouched for the accuracy of his work. Typically he would ask for a sketch plan of the

24

area where water was required. If he could find water there, the map would be returned with a red cross marking the spot. He would give instructions regarding how deep to dig and the quantity of water to be found. His book *Principles and Practice of Radiesthesia*[10] makes very interesting reading, and it was he who coined the term 'Radiesthesia', which means the determination of the presence of things by their radiations. He firmly believed that his dowsing was due to the detection of natural radiations, and it was because of this that he was able to gain the acceptance of his dowsing by the Roman Catholic Church.

Abbé Mermet dowsed for all sorts of things other than water and he was an avid experimenter. Many of his results were personal, like those of the late T.C. Lethbridge. This means that although the general method may work, different people discover different codes. For example, suppose you hold a pendulum over a gold ring. You have been told that gold has a certain 'rate' which will show up as a certain number of revolutions or swings of the pendulum. You try it and obtain ten clockwise rotations followed by fifteen anticlockwise rotations; after this the cycle repeats. This is your rate for gold. Both Abbé Mermet and Lethbridge believed that, because they obtained a certain result, this must be universal. Experiment has shown that this is not the case. My rate for gold and your rate may be quite different. This again is where the sceptic will point out the difference and say that this proves it is all rubbish. Not so. What matters is whether one's dowsing is accurate — not that one's codes are the same as everyone else's. And codes are what they are. This is like having an agreed code with someone else, but the only difference in this case is that the 'someone else' is a pendulum.

Tom Lethbridge, mentioned above, was an avid dowser who wrote about twenty years ago. His books make interest-

---

10. Mermet, Abbé, *Principles and Practice of Radiesthesia*, English Translation 1959, Vincent Stuart.

ing reading as he refused to talk to other dowsers about their methods. That way he felt he would discover the truth rather than be influenced by others. Unfortunately, as has been mentioned, he failed to appreciate that his coding methods might be personal, and this must be born in mind when reading any of his books or you can become disheartened when your codes do not agree with his.

So far we have looked mainly at mineral and water dowsing, which were the origins from which interest in dowsing has expanded this century. Medical and healing aspects of dowsing arose from this very practical background, and indeed it as well to keep the same down to earth approach to the healing aspects of dowsing if we are to avoid some serious pitfalls.

When considering medical dowsing, it is as well to remember that inside many people lurks a hypochondriac just waiting to get out. Dowsing can be a hypochondriac's delight: we can dowse to see if we are ill, what medicines we need, whether we are too ill to get up — the list is endless. This is why it is necessary to develop a sense of proportion and curb over-enthusiasm. Bear in mind in particular that it is all too easy to influence dowsing by personal preferences. Some people have caused much distress by seeing themselves as self-appointed guardians of the health of other people. There was one completely misguided person who wrote to people out of the blue saying that he had dowsed for their health. His diagnosis was nearly always that they had cancer and that he could help them. Such activities are not only quite unethical, but they also bring the whole practice of dowsing into serious question. These lunatic activities can undermine much patient and serious work by responsible practitioners.

The problem often arises not from deliberate malice but from overenthusiastic inexperienced dowsing, for what beginners often fail to appreciate, is that dowsing is under mental control. If one tries too hard, then the dowsing reactions can become far too sensitive. This is the problem

26

of becoming over-involved with the results.

In my early days of dowsing, I fell into just such a trap. I had been trying to find some land drains for Tony, who I mentioned earlier. He was having difficulties with a water-logged garden, owing to the builder having severed the land drains when the house was built. I found that I could find the land drains easily in the adjacent field and the farmer gave us permission to dig to prove my dowsing. There, sure enough, were the land drains. But I couldn't find the drains in Tony's garden. I had been using a sample of land drain (more about samples later) to help me in my search. As this had not worked I tried another tack — I would try to dowse for the small amount of water flowing in the drains. I went out into the field and started dowsing for very small water flows. I obtained a reaction from one of the land drains, but kept on walking to check over the next one. I then walked straight over a large underground stream. The pain was incredible. Both upper-arm muscles went into instantaneous total spasm. I forget what I said, but it was not suitable for people sensitive to bad language. I had wound my sensitivity up mentally in looking for small water flows, and this had caused the total over-reaction.

In dowsing for anything, it is easy for the beginner to try too hard, and thus achieve misleading if not painful results. For instance, virtually everyone has cancer cells in their bodies. These are not normally dangerous, as the body's auto-immune system will destroy or immobilise them as they are produced. However, dowsing for cancer with too much enthusiasm and too little experience can all too easily give a completely incorrect result. This is what, I suspect, happened in the case I mentioned previously. In dowsing, remember the Scottish saying and 'Gang warily'.

BRAIN RHYTHMS

So far we have been looking at dowsing and the effects of over-sensitivity. What about those people who claim not to be able to dowse? Particularly, what about the sceptic for whom nothing happens?

Firstly, we must remember what was mentioned earlier. The classical forked rod is difficult to hold correctly. This must have led to the idea that dowsing is a special gift, but this is not so, the dowsing ability is widespread. My first wife once tested two classes of children at her secondary school. The first class had just moved up from middle school. She showed them how to dowse with angle-rods and then sent them out into the playground. (Just what the headmaster thought of this I never discovered.) She found that only a few children had no response but over 80 per cent experienced a good reaction and could follow where the drains to the school and playing field ran. She then checked with a class of sixth-formers. Most of them did obtain positive reactions, but the number not experiencing reactions was now about 40 per cent. In other words, there were about twice as many non-dowsers in the sixth form. Why? There could have been several reasons but the most likely one was that of an increasing scepticism that often sets in as children get older. Attitude of mind would therefore appear to have an important bearing on the ability to dowse.

The late and much loved Max Cade, a remarkable teacher of meditation, once did an interesting experiment. Max was a great believer in the use of biofeedback techniques to help people with meditation. (Incidentally this work is now being carried on by his wife Isobel Maxwell Cade). Max had been training some of his students to be able to maintain the brain in the relaxed alpha-rhythm state while keeping their eyes open. The students were able to walk about with an alpha-monitor that gave a tone in an earpiece as long as they remained in an alpha-state. He took from each of them something personal, like a ring or a watch, and asked them to leave the room. He then hid their objects under newspapers on a long table. They were then asked to come back into the room, maintaining their alpha state, and slowly 'scan' over the table with their hands. Without exception, the alpha rhythms cut off when their hands were over their own personal belongings. When questioned, none of them was aware at a conscious level that anything had happened to them. All they were aware of was that the tone in their earpiece had stopped at that point.

So far as is known, dowsing can first be detected in the brain rhythms. As alpha brain activity is associated with a state of mental relaxation, the cessation of the alpha rhythm indicates an increased level of mental tension. This in turn can lead to increased muscle tension, and it is changes in muscle tension that move angle-rods and the forked rod. As brain activity can change without necessarily affecting muscle balance (between the flexor and extensor muscle tensions), this will explain why some people cannot dowse with instruments such as angle-rods. It appears, however, that even with those people, providing they can relax sufficiently, the dowsing response can show up in the spectrum of their brain activity.

As well as giving over-sensitivity in some people, trying too hard will inhibit the dowsing response in others. What is needed to be successful in dowsing, is to be detached from the results that may be obtained. Autosuggestion and anxiety are the permanent enemies of the dowser. For this reason, it is suggested that where the results of dowsing are important to a dowser, then he or she should seriously consider finding someone else to do the dowsing for them. It is one thing having dowsing reactions, something quite different in being accurate in those reactions.

In the next chapter I will be describing the tools of the trade, the different dowsing methods available and their possible pitfalls. Not everyone is comfortable with one particular method of dowsing, some people get no response from a pendulum, others cannot use a forked rod. The main thing is to experiment and to find what *you* are comfortable with. Some books are full of all sorts of mumbo-jumbo: you must do this or not do that. Forget all this. There are as many ways of dowsing as there are dowsers. Many people start off with one well-defined way and then adapt it for their own way of working. That is fine and is by far the best way. The main thing is to keep an open mind and try it out for yourself, for ultimately only you can prove its validity and know how it can best serve you.

CHAPTER 3

TOOLS OF THE TRADE

Although the pendulum is most suited to medical dowsing, traditional instruments, such as the forked stick and angle-rods, have their advantages in certain situations. They can also be used to master basic dowsing techniques, such as checking for underground water flows, before more subtle applications can be attempted.

'It is simple, or it is nothing.' *Evelyn Penrose*

Evelyn Penrose was an expert dowser from Cornwall and her book *Adventure Unlimited* (now alas out of print) makes fascinating reading. She worked all over the world, often for mining companies. Her main point was that dowsing is essentially simple and should be kept that way. With that I would totally agree, and this is why you will find no complex methods given in this book. Every attempt has been made to keep things simple, as it is within complexity that we lose our way.

Over the years there have been many dowsing tools developed. Many of these have had temporary acceptance, and then fallen into disuse. The first thing that should be born in mind is that there is much folklore, still, about dowsing tools. I well remember one lady who looked admiringly at a beechwood pendulum that I was using. 'That's a lovely pendulum,' she said, 'It's so important to use natural materials for accurate results. What sort of thread are you using? It looks like silk.' 'Well actually', I replied, 'it's made of Nylon.' After that I felt that I had been consigned to the ranks of the inaccurate dowsers.

As was mentioned earlier, the reaction is on the body of the dowser, not on the rod or pendulum being used. I would agree that it is far better to feel at home with the tools that you use, and it is irrelevant what you actually use for your dowsing. What matters is, does it work for you? I have a treasured memory from a Congress of the British Society of Dowsers at Harrogate. There had been an afternoon of dowsing at Fountains Abbey, and a group of us had gone into a tea-shop in Ripon for afternoon tea. One of the group decided to dowse over the scones to see if they would disagree with her. She opened her handbag and produced from it a toy mouse. She then held it up by its tail and used it as a pendulum. It demonstrated that one really can use anything, but this incident would hardly instil confidence into a sceptical onlooker!

At the same congress, one of the members produced a set of angle-rods and defied anyone to dowse with them. They were made with gimbal bearings in the handles, so that whatever one did with one's wrists, the rods pointed in the same direction. Several people who firmly believed that the dowsing force was on the rods tried to use them. Much to their annoyance, the rods refused to work at all; obstinately pointing in the same direction all the time. I tried them, and found it quite strange, knowing that the rods should be moving, but with nothing at all happening to them.

If then one bears in mind that it is a muscular reaction on the body, rather than a force directly on the tool being used, it is possible to begin to see how dowsing tools work, and much of the mysticism and elitism from dowsing can be removed, an achievement that will help us to view the dowsing tools in an objective manner.

Consider the forked stick first, as it seems to have been the first recorded dowsing tool. The stick need not be wood; plastic or thin metal bent to the correct shape will do just as well. If you try with wood, it is important to select a nice 'vee' branch of supple wood. Hazel is the classical wood,

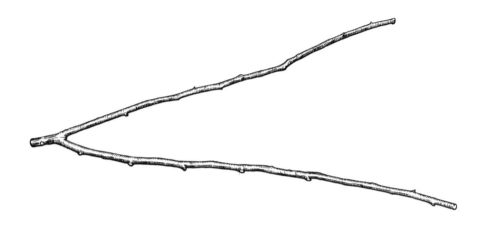

Figure 5a. Classical forked hazel rod

but rhododendron, dogwood, and other strong flexible woods are good. If in doubt, try it and see but note that brittle or too flexible woods will either break or collapse in your hands. It is important how the stick is held. Figure 5a shows a typical forked rod and Figure 5b shows how it is held. The palms are upwards and the stick is spring-loaded by the outer parts of the fork being bent open from their natural position. This can be seen by comparing the shape of the rod in the two illustrations. When holding a forked rod this way, which may feel unnatural to the beginner, any rotation of the forearms will make the rod move. If the tops of the forearms rotate towards each other, the tip of the rod will dip. Conversely, if the tops of the arms move away from each other, the rod tip will rise. Angling the wrists to increase or decrease the spring-loading of the rod will increase or decrease the sensitivity of the rod. Too much tension in the rod will either make it unstable so it jumps up or down on its own, or it will break, hence the importance of a suitable material for the rod.

33

Figure 5b. Method of holding a forked rod with the palms pointing upward

Having mastered holding a forked rod, the next thing is to try it out. Really the best place for this is out in the open country away from prying eyes. Most people experience quite a strong reaction from underground water flows, and there is something natural and fundamental about using a forked rod to look for water in the countryside. However, for the majority this may not be easy to arrange. Alternatively, like me, you could try looking for such things as drains, gas and water pipes. What one is looking for is a reaction from the rod, either up or down. Never mind which way it moves, or wondering whether it is going in the right direction: there is no right direction. What matters is that it moves in a repeatable manner. If it moves every time at a certain place, and you don't know what is there, never mind; we will be looking later at methods of analysis. At this stage it is a matter of experiencing movements and increasing confidence.

34

But suppose that there is no suitable material for a forked rod where you live. What then? You can make a suitable rod from two long bits of plastic bound together at one end — long thin plastic knitting needles have been used by some people. Whalebone from Victorian corsets was once popular, but thankfully whalebone is no longer available. Basically, two pieces of anything springy that can be bound together at one end are suitable for use. However, it can be quite difficult to hold such rods correctly.

Suppose that you find the forked rod too difficult to use, or perhaps you get no response at all, what then? Perhaps the next dowsing instrument to try is the angle-rod. Although the pendulum is more widely used for healing applications, it is much more susceptible to autosuggestion. Angle-rods have a nice solid feel to them, and can be used for healing work if the pendulum does not work for you, even though the pendulum is easier to use. Also there is something to be said for locating such physical things as water and pipes before venturing into the rather more difficult areas.

Angle-rods are very simple to make, and need consist of nothing more than two bent pieces of wire. The diameter and length of the wire is not too critical. Large sparkler wires left after bonfire night will even do at a pinch. It is best to use fairly thick wire so that the rods are not seriously affected by light winds. A diameter of about 2 mm will do well, and before bending, the wire lengths should be about 30 cm. Each wire should then be bent at right angles about 9 cm from one end. Also the wire is best made from a heavy metal such as steel to prevent it being too sensitive to the wind. The wire in steel (not aluminium) coat-hangers is fine when straightened out. The rods are then held, one in each hand, with the longer length of the 'L' pointing forward. The rods must only be held lightly so that they are free to swing. If this is found to be too difficult, then hollow handles can be used. Instead of the bamboo that I mentioned earlier, I find that it is neater to use old cheap ball-point pens. The Bic ones are ideal. If the innards of such pens are pulled out with a pair of pliers, then hollow handles with a bottom plastic bung are formed. Again the shorter length of the 'L' needs to be just a little bit longer than the holder so that the rods do not foul the tops of the tubes. The rods can be dropped into these holders and the pens then held instead of the rods (see Fig. 6).

I use angle-rods that I made myself with ball-races in the handles. This enables me to use thick brass horizontal rods of about 3 mm diameter. These are easy to hold, and operate well in all but strong winds. Apart from that, they also look more professional than bent welding wires, even though the latter will work just as well on a calm day.

Learning to walk with angle-rods can be quite difficult. The art is to walk slowly without jolting the rods, keeping the front of the rods dropped down slightly. If the rod tips are above the horizontal, then inevitably the rods will swing round back towards you. Indeed the best way of controlling the sensitivity of the rods is by adjusting how far the tips of the rods are below the horizontal.

If the rods are initially parallel, then for most people when walking over an underground feature, the tips of the rods will move towards each other. For a few people the rods move apart, so if the rods move apart for you, then there is nothing to worry about. Please don't think that your 'polarity' is reversed or that you are suffering from incorrect diet or ley lines! It is simply that people react differently, nothing more.

What drives the angle-rods is exactly the same as for the forked rod — a slight unconscious rotation of the forearms. If the tops of the forearms rotate towards each other, then the rods will move towards each other; a movement away will cause the rods to move out. It is the change in balance between the flexor and extensor muscles that makes the rods move. If your rods move outwards, it means that the change in muscular balance just happens to have a net result that is the opposite direction to the majority of people, nothing else.

36

Figure 6. Angle-rods with ball-point pen holders, showing position of rods when something has been located

Most people experience a reaction with angle-rods, unless they are totally convinced that it will not work. Often the reaction is initially small and may be hard to see. However, perseverance pays off. Initially my angle-rod reactions were small and only just noticeable. Within a year they were strong, but it needed practice to gain the confidence that was necessary to give such positive results. I was sceptical when I first tried dowsing and there is no doubt that it adversely affected my dowsing sensitivity at the beginning.

Like the forked rod, it is useful, though by no means essential, to try angle-rods out in the countryside. Angle-rods have rather more versatility than the forked rod, which soon becomes evident with use. Suppose that you are looking for water, and unknown to you there is an underground aquifer (this is the academically correct name for an underground stream) running parallel to the direction that you are walking. Under these conditions the rods will often both move and point to the side of you where the water is flowing, thus showing that the nearest water is to one side of you, rather than in front. This can save a lot of leg-work at times.

THE PENDULUM

There are other forms of rods, but they are of little importance except for some specialised uses where they may be helpful. The pendulum can be made of any material; what matters is that its operator feels at home with it. A fairly heavy finger ring on a piece of cotton thread will work well for many people. Some dowsers use metal pendulums on metal chains, others crystal pendulums on fine silver or gold chains, others use wooden or plastic pendulums. The main point is that the pendulum bob needs to be sufficiently heavy so that its movements can be felt by the fingers. An attractive nickel-plated brass pendulum can be obtained from the British Society of Dowsers, whose address is given in Appendix 1 (see page 174).

Again, it is an unconscious movement of the hand that makes the instrument move. In this case the pendulum is given small imperceptible pushes from the hand at the same rate as the natural frequency of oscillation of the pendulum. For this reason, many people find that there is a certain length of string to the pendulum that gives the best response. A satisfactory way of determining the optimum length is to start by using a short thread of between 5 to 8 centimetres in length. The pendulum can then be successively lengthened until the most sensitive results are obtained.

One way of getting used to the pendulum is to 'tell' it to go in, say, a clockwise direction. The pendulum may then begin to rotate in that direction without any conscious physical intervention. For more speedy results the pendulum can initially be swung in a straight line before telling it what to do. This action of the mind in being able to unconsciously alter the swing of a pendulum has been known for a long time, and it is often used to argue that dowsing is therefore wishful thinking. This effect must always be borne in mind, as it shows just how easy it is for wishful thinking to influence one's dowsing. This effect can occur whatever dowsing implement is used, but it tends to be more noticeable with a pendulum.

Checking for underground water flows with a pendulum can be done, but it is not as easy as with angle-rods or a forked rod. It is a matter of walking slowly along and watching for the pendulum to either start moving or change its mode of movement. For instance, it may change from a straight-line swing to moving with a circular swing. The main difficulty is that the action of walking tends to move the pendulum, so one has to walk very steadily and carefully for the results to be unambiguous.

The pendulum is more useful for indoor use, and as it only needs one hand it is easy to use. Also, it is capable of even more responses than the angle-rods, as we shall see. This make it useful for healing applications as it can give more graded answers than 'yes' or 'no'.

Having looked at the main dowsing instruments and how

they operate, we can now look at how they can be used in practical circumstances. The next chapter is concerned with how to dowse practically, and the pitfalls that may be encountered. And pitfalls there are. On the water-finding level, I have experienced that feeling of wishing the earth would swallow me up, for when someone has excavated 8 metres down for water, on your say-so, and has found nothing, it is a most awful feeling. Telling them that you have succeeded 99 per cent of the time in the past is of no help whatever. To you a 1 per cent failure may seem to be a very low failure rate, but that 99 per cent success rate means nothing to the person with the dry hole.

Not that I would wish to put anyone off from trying out dowsing, far from it. I simply wish to point out that one has a responsibility to those for whom you may dowse. Whether you charge a fee or not for your services is irrelevant but some people, amateurs of the worst kind, do not charge as they then feel that they can avoid responsibility for their results that way. This is as irresponsible as someone I know who gives clairvoyant readings to people and disclaims responsibility when things do not turn out as predicted. 'That was the "other me" that was talking,' you are told. No, if we are to give advice to others, it is vital to be as competent as is humanly possible. Exaggerating one's abilities will inevitably lead to trouble later on.

So let's have a look at the methods that can be used in dowsing. Carefully used they will enable the prospective dowser to become more and more proficient without the risk of embarrassing failures.

CHAPTER 4

USING THE TOOLS

In learning to dowse it is essential to understand what the responses you obtain mean — and what the pitfalls are in interpreting them. The use of samples and coding methods can help, including appropriate rulers and the 'Mager Rosette', a reliable tool for determining water purity. Another method of analysis is based on the 'question and answer' technique.

The tool that is the most widely used for healing applications of dowsing is the pendulum. Nevertheless, sometimes it is useful to be able to use either the angle-rods or the forked rod. Therefore, although most of this chapter will refer to the use of the pendulum, the other tools must not be forgotten. Sometimes they are much more suitable for a particular type of dowsing.

When trying dowsing outside for the first time, many people ask this question: 'I have just found something by dowsing, but what is it?' This is the main problem after finding that dowsing works: discovering just what the dowsing reactions mean. Just because dowsing rods move when walking over a particular place tells you nothing about what lies underground. It may be water, or a pipe, or mine shafts, or virtually anything. Exactly the same problem applies to the healing applications of dowsing. The vitally important thing is to know what you have found. It is of little help to say to someone who is ill that you cannot get the correct treatment by your dowsing — but you have confirmed that they are ill!

It was mentioned earlier that coding methods are used to

obtain the information that we need. These coding methods are necessary, but can be a major pitfall unless one goes warily. For example, there was a firm in Leeds that made an instrument called the Revealer. This was a pair of 'tarted-up' angle-rods, one of them having a set of sample materials attached to it. The samples were of common underground things such as drain-pipe, copper, coal, etc. I tried a pair out and found that they worked beautifully. When I pulled the copper sample towards me I could find our copper feed pipe to the central heating; the drain-pipe sample gave me just the drains, and so on. I then read the instructions carefully (when all else fails read the instructions) and found that I had got it all wrong. According to the book, holding the copper sample should have found everything *but* copper. The same was true for all the other samples and I had been working the rods in reverse, as it were. In other words, my own ideas had completely overridden what the manufacturer had said should happen, and I was working the completely opposite way round!

Further light is shed on this occurrence by something that happened to me just a little later on. A Mr Gutteridge contacted me via the British Society of Dowsers and asked me if he could demonstrate his angle-rods to me, as they were much better than the Revealer. He duly came round to see me and showed me an impressive pair of rods with dials that could be set up for the material to be found. He demonstrated their use outside in the garden. They worked fine; he was able to locate our underground stream and identify it correctly. We then went inside. 'Look,' he said, 'I will show you just how sensitive these rods are. I will set them to a very unusual material and then find it with them.' He twiddled the dials and set off from our dining room into the hall. He had never been inside the house before so he knew nothing of what was there. As he walked into the hall his rods swung off to the right, and round the corner they pointed to our wall barometer. 'There you are,' he said, 'I set them to mercury!'

I hadn't the heart to tell him that the barometer was an aneroid one which had no mercury in it, and the thermometer in it used spirit, not mercury. If his dowsing had worked accurately the rods would have pointed the opposite way into the bathroom, where there was a mercury clinical thermometer. I am sure that fixed in his mind was the image of a barometer, and that he certainly found. If I had been a sceptic, rather than an experienced dowser, that demonstration would have completely destroyed any credibility that he had built up with his dowsing outside.

This then is the key factor with all dowsing, namely that the attitude of mind is all-important. I will describe how certain coding methods can be used, and useful they can be, but remember at all times that the whole thing is under mental control. *Wishful thinking destroys accuracy.*

In outside work it is important to be able to determine the depth of a stream or other object that has been located by dowsing. There are two methods that have widespread acceptance and which at first sight would appear to be based on natural effects.

The 'Bishop's Rule' for finding the depth of a stream or an object is straightforward. It is based on the idea that if an underground water flow is at a certain depth, say 6 metres, then parallel with the line of the stream and 6 metres away from each side of it on the surface, one can locate dowsing lines of influence. The basic method of depthing is therefore as follows.

First locate the line of a stream and peg it out to determine on the surface the line of its flow. Then, starting off by standing immediately above the stream, walk away from it at right angles to its flow, until the rod moves again. Mark this spot. The distance away of this marker from the line of the stream on the surface is equal to the depth of the stream. This principle is shown in Figure 7.

Using this simple method makes it easy to determine the depth of the stream. However, there are problems. One does not necessarily obtain the correct value for depth.

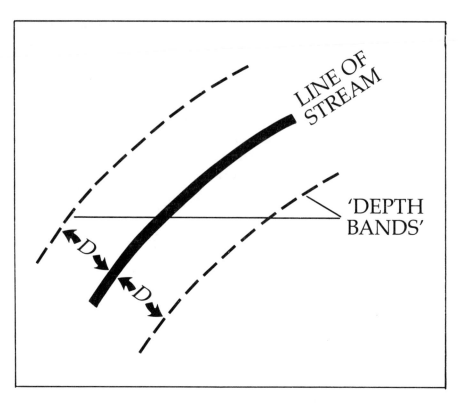

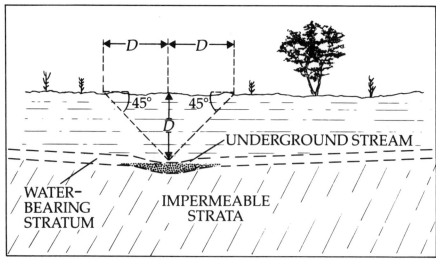

Figure 7. The 'Bishop's Rule' (see text on p. 43). This can be used for locating the depth of an underground stream or object

Also, how does one cope with the problem where one just cannot walk far enough sideways without falling off a cliff?

A varient of the Bishop's Rule (incidentally, no-one seems to know who Bishop or The Bishop was) is the 'point-depth method.' In the point-depth method one uses a magnetic-rod marker driven into the ground immediately above the stream. This is said to convert the 'depth-bands' into a circle, so that one can walk out in any direction to find a reaction that is equal to the depth of the stream. A Major Creyke once went so far as to use a Mumetal (a very expensive and magnetically sensitive material) rod to obtain accurate results. One member of the BSD at a congress walked several miles on a field trip carrying a heavy crowbar that he used for point-depth testing!

What matters most is the particular method you have in your mind. If you expect to find depth bands, then it is most likely that you will find them. If you walk away from your marker over a stream in any direction, expecting to find a reaction at a distance away equal to the depth of the stream, then most likely that is what you will find.

If you locate anything underground by dowsing, then you can always use the point-depth method to determine its depth. Just put a marker immediately above the located object and continue dowsing away from that point in any convenient direction. What one needs to have in mind is the statement, 'Let the rods move when I am at a distance away from the marker equal to the depth of the object that I have found.' Walk slowly and carefully, but without trying to make anything happen. Mark the ground where the rods move by their maximum amount. All being well, the distance from this second marker to the first one will be equal to the depth of the underground object.

It is important to be careful. Particularly it is important that one gains practice with checking the depth of objects whose depth is known or can be ascertained. It is all too easy to have too much faith in a particular method — for instance some people believe that the point-depth and

Bishop's Rule methods are based on physical radiations and are therefore infallible. I know to my cost that it is not always so, as sometimes I find quite a strong reaction at a distance corresponding to half the actual depth. This can be unfortunate to say the least, and was the reason why I had a 3-metre deep hole in the lawn of a previous house of mine, not a well, which is what it was meant to be, just a deep hole! The water was actually 6 metres down, as reference to the local geological map would have told me if I had looked at it before, rather than after the digging. The moral is to check one's dowsing carefully when beginning, and to be careful of over-confidence later on.

CODING METHODS

Starting with the pendulum, what sort of coding methods should be used and how reliable are they?

One of the simplest methods is to use a ruler. A 100-cm (1-metre) rule is fine for those who like mathematical accuracy, as it will give a reading directly in per cent. Actually a foot rule works just as well and is rather more convenient. Put some item of food at the 'high' end of the rule (30 cm or 12 in) and start off with your pendulum at the zero end. The idea is that the nearer to the high end of the rule that your pendulum reacts, the better the food will be for you. If it reacts straightaway, then the food is definitely harmful to you and should not be eaten. A reading should be over half-way up the scale before the food is acceptable as an item of diet. As a beginner it is vital that you take any results with a large pinch of salt (not literally!). You *may* be correct if your dowsing tells you that cream buns are 100 per cent right for you, but personally I would doubt it, as wishful thinking can so easily affect the answer.

What sort of reaction should the pendulum give? One simple way is to just hold the pendulum and ask it the question, 'Show me which movement indicates a positive answer.' For many people this proves to be a clockwise circle when viewed from above. This is the method that I always recommend. It may take time for the pendulum to move, and if so give it a small backward and forward swing and watch to see if it changes into a circle. Above all, don't be disheartened if nothing much happens at first. For some people it takes a bit of practice before the pendulum moves at all reliably. After all, you are trying to forge a neuro-muscular link with the intuitive part of the brain, so don't get impatient if nothing much happens at first, and don't become tense trying, nothing inhibits dowsing more than tension. A small amount of alcohol can help one to relax, but try to avoid becoming like one dowser who could only dowse accurately when he was very drunk.

Suppose that you now obtain a definite pendulum movement which indicates a positive dowsing answer. This is equivalent to the angle-rods crossing or the forked stick lifting. The pendulum, however, has many movements available. It can swing in straight lines at varying angles, it can make ellipses at varying angles both clockwise and anticlockwise, also clockwise and anticlockwise circles. In other words there is the capability for it to indicate more than just a 'yes' response, and this is the key to its use in healing applications.

Holding the pendulum by its string, ask it to indicate what movement indicates negative or 'no'. For many people this is an anticlockwise circle, but again don't be surprised if you find something different. If you now obtain two clearly different movements, then you can check food without a rule, but with no real idea of how good or bad it is for you. Hold the pendulum over foods with the mental question, 'Is this food good for me to eat?'

You can get surprises with either 'yes' or 'no' answers. I once demonstrated dowsing at a theatre bar to some friends. I dowsed over a pint of beer and, much to my surprise, I found a clear 'yes' answer. This was not what I had been expecting at all, and caused a lot of amusement as

I had been telling them how beer was bad for me and that it would show up as bad with my dowsing. The result could have been due to the vitamin B content of the beer, as I could well have been suffering from a vitamin B deficiency that day. This shows again how careful one has to be to avoid generalisations.

There was one very positive thing that came out of that particular demonstration. If your dowsing can give you surprises like that — giving results that are totally unexpected — then it shows that autosuggestion is not overriding the dowsing faculty. It indicates that your dowsing is getting to the point, even if not completely there, where it can always be relied on.

If your positive and negative responses are too similar, then what do you do? In this case the best advice that I know of is to be firm. Decide which response needs changing and decide what you want it to be in future. State very clearly what your new 'yes' or 'no' is going to be, and then practise it. Adopting the same approach to training a dog, you ask it to 'Show me my new "no",' and praise 'it' when it goes the way that you have chosen. You are virtually reprogramming a reflex, so it may take a little time but I can assure you that it works.

Over homoeopathic medicines I used to obtain a 'no' response for the ones which were necessary for a patient. Presumably this was because in high doses the medicine would have caused the symptoms that the patient was suffering from. This was a nuisance and one day I became fed up with my 'no' response meaning yes. I therefore told myself that from that day on my dowsing response for *any* medicine would be 'yes' when it was needed. It worked like a charm and I have never had any difficulty since.

You will have noticed that I asked you to have a question in mind when checking over an item of food for a yes or no response. The question was, 'Is this food good for me?' This is part of the code. Without the question, the dowsing becomes meaningless. You might be dowsing for whether the food had grown in good soil, or indeed for water under the ground under the food. This method of dowsing is sometimes called 'Question and Answer' because there is always a question in the mind of the dowser, sometimes implied rather than stated. Of all the dowsing methods it is the most powerful, as it is only limited by the questions that can be asked. Nevertheless, it needs to be used with care, and for many people a more disciplined method may be better, certainly to start with. However, before looking at more 'mathematical' coding methods, let us complete our examination of possible communications from the pendulum.

So far the starting position, most likely at rest or swinging in a straight line, that indicates neutral has been established, and the different movements for 'yes' and 'no' have also been determined. Suppose we ask a question that has incorrect implications like, 'Should I include this item in my diet?' The correct answer may be, 'yes, but. . . '. In other words a qualified yes or no. The pendulum must therefore be left an escape route to let the dowser know that a question has been asked that has necessary implications. Perhaps, on diet matters, it is quite satisfactory to eat a certain item but not accompanied by some particular foods, so two more indications, 'yes-but' and 'no-but', are needed to show that there is other information that has to be gained.

All one needs is to ask the pendulum to give those indications. Just for the record, my indications are straight-line for neutral, anticlockwise ellipse for no-but, anticlockwise circle for no, clockwise ellipse for yes-but, and clockwise circle for yes. Again it takes time to check such movements and become confident with them, so never be in a hurry.

Suppose that you now have a set of pendulum movements that you can reliably interpret, from a pure yes right through to a pure no. How can you use these results? Take as an example the case of having located an underground stream. It is little use being able to say that there is water to be found at a certain place without being able to give any idea as to whether it is drinkable or not. It is often forgotten that underground water supplies are not always pure. They can be heavily mineralised and so be unfit to drink. In looking next at one of the coding methods that can be used for determining water purity, I will also show how simple a basic coding method can be.

It was a Frenchman called Henri Mager who gave dowsing a simple yet reliable tool for determining water purity. The device is called the 'Mager Rosette'. It is a circular disk that is split up into eight equal sectors. These sectors are coloured violet, blue, green, yellow, red, grey, black and white, in that order. The disk is usually about ten centimetres in diameter, but the size is not important. I often use one made from plastic because it is more durable, but one made from thick card with the segments painted in will work just as well. The appearance of the rosette is shown in Figure 8. When using the pendulum, the colour in use is selected by holding the appropriate segment between a finger and thumb of one hand whilst using the other hand to dowse with a pendulum. The standard meaning of the colours is as follows.

Violet — absolutely pure water, the best spring water obtainable.
Blue — normal drinking water, for example tap water, not as good for one as the violet type, but still drinkable.
Green — some types of mineralisation present, such as copper.
Yellow — hard water, also water containing other salts such as magnesium.
Red — iron content, for example chalybeate springs will give a response on this colour.
Grey — polluted water, also if the water contains lead.
Black — so-called 'Black Streams'. These are water flows that can seriously affect the health of people living above them. This is referred to later on in the book (see pp. 142–7).

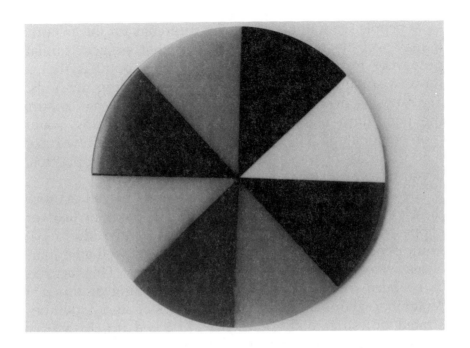

Figure 8. The Mager Rosette

White — this colour is that of many of the reputed healing springs and also occurs where there is dissolved silver in the water.

These are the predominant meanings of the colours in the rosette, although they are not the only ones, so if an underground stream of water has been discovered, then it is possible to determine its purity from which colours a reaction is obtained. It is simply a matter of holding a colour between finger and thumb in one hand and seeing, when standing over the water flow, whether the pendulum gives a positive response. If a response is obtained on blue and yellow, the water will be drinkable, but hard. The amplitude of swing of the pendulum with the yellow colour will give some idea of the degree of hardness, in this particular case.

The meanings of the colours are not absolute, although

most people seem to obtain similar meanings for the colours. It may well be that it is the colours that suggest similar properties to people. However, the main point is that it forms a suitable starting point to look at coding methods. Try dowsing over standard tap water and see what colours the pendulum reacts to. Then try bottled spring water (non-carbonated). Then try iron water. Leaving a few rusty nails in a glass of water for a day or two should supply this, if you have no natural iron-water spring nearby.

The rosette can be used for solid materials as well as those dissolved in water. Try dowsing over a piece of lead or copper, for instance, and see what colours give the maximum pendulum reaction. Solid materials as well as mineralised water will give you positive responses. This fact has to be born in mind, as it can be misleading at times. I remember giving a lecture in Manchester and I demonstrated dowsing to the audience. I picked up, in a very limited space, a straight-line feature. Using the rosette I obtained reactions to the colours grey and yellow. 'Most likely a stream of polluted hard water,' I said, 'about two metres down'. The depth I obtained by the point-depth method mentioned previously. 'Could the colours mean anything else?' asked the Chairman. 'Yes,' I answered hesitantly, 'grey can be lead, and yellow can be from calcium-rich materials such as limestone boulders or bones.' 'You may be interested', he replied, 'in knowing that this building is built over a medieval cemetery, and that there are still skeletons underneath here in lead-lined coffins!' So it looked as if I had dowsed accurately, but my interpretation was incorrect due to my inferring that the line that I had found was due to a water flow.

The rosette can also be used with angle-rods by holding the rosette with finger and thumb of one hand, and using the remaining fingers to hold the rod, not easy, but quite possible.

The rosette is therefore a simple, but obviously restricted form of communication code. For its original purpose of determining water purity, it is usually quite sufficiently

52

accurate. Something capable of giving a much greater amount of discrimination is needed, however, if the dowser is to be capable of analysing complex materials or situations.

The use of samples is one such method that can be expanded to meet virtually any need. The only limitation to this method is the number of samples that may be needed. Take the problem of trying to find a lead pipe outside in a garden where there may be electricity cables, gas pipes, etc. How can one be certain of what has been found? One way, having found a reaction that looks as if it could be the required pipe, is to then check with a lead sample. Using angle-rods, a small lead sample can be held in one hand along with one of the rods. Using a pendulum is easier, as the sample can be held with the opposite hand to the pendulum. Some pendulums are made that are hollow for sample use. One simply opens the pendulum bob, puts the sample inside, and then screws the bob back together again.

This method of dowsing is sometimes called 'using the property of affinities'. The idea is that there is an affinity between materials of the same sort, and that is why this method of selective dowsing succeeds. Unfortunately for those looking for an easy explanation, this is not the case. I remember someone making up a whole set of sealed samples and giving them to some dowsers to try out. They worked well, the dowsers locating copper wires with the copper samples, lead pipes with the lead samples, and so on. It was only after the test that the maker of the samples owned-up — the samples were not what they were labelled. He had swapped the labels between the samples, so copper could well have been labelled lead, and so on.

This is not to decry the use of samples, not at all. When in difficulties I will still use samples, even after more than twenty years of dowsing. The main point is that *the mind can override whatever system we are using.*

So beware of trying too hard. No system can cope with the over-enthusiastic dowser, and this is often where inaccuracies occur.

Samples can be used for medical dowsing purposes. This will be dealt with in later chapters. Indeed some firms can supply samples of viruses in very low concentrations, bacteria and even diseased organs (again in very small concentrations!) for analysis purposes. Such samples come in sealed glass vials and do not need to be opened.

So basically there are two fundamentally different methods of analysis: one uses a method of coding, such as the Mager Rosette or samples, and the other is based on asking questions and seeing what answer one obtains from the dowsing implement. In the next chapter I will look further into these different methods of analysis and explain how to get started with them.

CHAPTER 5

FOOD ALLERGIES AND SENSITIVITIES

An application of dowsing which brings immediate personal benefit is the discovery of personal food allergies and sensitivities — conversely this technique can be an excellent method for checking the accuracy of your dowsing.

The most difficult part of dowsing is getting started. The most common question that comes is always, 'How do I start and what can I dowse for?' As described in the last chapter, the first thing is to obtain movements from whatever dowsing implement you decide to use. For health and healing applications the pendulum is the best tool because of its various possible responses. However, if a pendulum refuses to work, then angle-rods can be used.

When dowsing, bear in mind that it is possible to be affected by the presence of other people, so it is best to be kind to yourself and start off by working alone. There is no point making things more difficult than they need be. I had heard how the presence of other people upset some dowsers, so I once carried out a test to see just how true this was for me. I asked a friend, Hilary, to help me and proceeded to dowse over an underground stream in my garden. I purposely allowed myself to be open to her thoughts, if such a thing was possible. I dowsed over the stream, away from her, to see what I discovered. The results were amazing. If she wanted me to get results, then the rods moved in my hands; if she mentally said 'no' then I found no response whatever. This worked repeatedly even though I had no idea of what she was thinking at the time of my dowsing. The implications are — be *very, very careful*. Onlookers *can* affect your dowsing if you are open to their influence. Play safe and practise on your own.

Let us assume that you now have a pendulum that works satisfactorily so that you have known 'yes' and 'no' responses. Put out on a table a whole set of different foods, including herbs, spices and drinks, anything that you may eat or drink. Write their names down on a piece of paper and then systematically check each one of them by dowsing with the question in your mind, 'Is this item good for me to eat (or drink)?' Write down your results against the names on the paper, noting any 'yes-but' and 'no-but' answers. These answers often indicate that such food will be suitable or unsuitable under certain conditions.

If for any reason you can only work with, say, angle-rods, then place the item on the floor and check it by walking over it. In this case a positive response will mean that it is good. You may find the rods swinging outwards for a 'no' response and partially in or out for 'yes-but' and 'no-but' responses.

Use items from different sources that are otherwise the same. For instance, try several different brands of tea or coffee as they are not all the same. For example, some brands of instant coffee are made in stainless steel equipment, some in aluminium.

Have a good look at the list. Are there any surprises? If all is what you would have expected, then you should be cautious. Often we are the most attached to the food items that we are the most allergic to. Food allergies, or food sensitivities as they are sometimes called, can be a good way of checking one's dowsing. The question that you should have had in mind previously was, 'Is this food (or drink) good for me?' Now change the question to, 'Am I allergic to this food?' There is a subtle difference between these two

56

questions. One substance may be poisonous to you, i.e. toxic, without causing allergic responses.

Repeat your dowsing with the same items and the changed question and see what answers you get. Incidentally it is a good idea to keep the first results out of sight and just keep your mind on the dowsing. At this stage you are seeking to gain experience, not trying to prove anything.

Compare your answers. Are they the same? Do they indeed appear to conflict? Is something good for you but yet you appear to be allergic to it? In this latter case, please don't assume that your dowsing is no good. It may be that you are only weakly allergic to something, and there is something within the item whose 'good' properties outweigh the allergic negative characteristics.

If you now wish to check the second set of responses, there is a way that works for the majority of people. This is based on the pulse test for allergies. The pioneering work in this area was done in America, and the books of Dr Arthur Coca[11] give an excellent description of the subject and its importance to health. In this country, the work was taken up shortly after the American results were published, and Dr Mackarness's book, *Not All In The Mind*[12], is perhaps the best known popular book on the subject. In both countries the pulse test was found to work for the majority of people, and it can be an effective analytical tool.

The test is carried out as follows. Take your pulse on first waking up after a night's sleep, counting the beats for one whole minute. Then get up, and before eating check it again. It should be lowest on waking and then increase by a small amount, say five beats per minute after getting up. If these figures are the other way round, the pulse rate falling after getting up, then you may well be allergic to the house-

11.   Coca, Arthur F., MD, *The Pulse Test: Easy Allergy Detection*, Arco, 1972.

12.   Mackarness, Dr Richard, *Not All In The Mind*, Pan Books, 1976.

dust mite that lives in bedding. Incidentally, *don't brush your teeth before this test, you may be allergic to the toothpaste!*

Then eat one single item of food from your dowsed list and wait five minutes. Check your pulse again. If the pulse rate has risen by more than about five beats per minute, then it is highly probable that you are allergic to that particular food. You can do this with single foods before a normal meal, and it will often sort out major allergic reactions. This is not the whole story, however, as some minor allergic reactions can be masked by the major ones for quite a long period of time. For instance, if you have a major allergic response to the bread that you eat, and you eat it every day, then it may completely mask minor allergens in food until you have fasted for several days.

However, all that is sought is some corroboration for your dowsing, and you need not be worried about the exactitudes of food allergy detection at this point. The main thing is to see if there is some relationship between the two sets of results. Food sensitivities are important, however. For some people they can create a continuous drain of energy and have a debilitating effect. It is worth remembering that we are often allergic to the things that we like the most. For instance, I am personally not allergic to tobacco. I can smoke a cigarette and my pulse rate remains virtually the same. Equally I get no 'kick' out of smoking, so I have no desire to smoke and therefore never normally do so. Addiction and allergic response often go hand-in-hand. A close relative of mine had ulcerative colitis when he was a teenager and was being threatened with a possible colostomy. Fortunately, we were able to establish that he was allergic to milk (all milk, not just cow's milk), and this was a major causative factor. The interesting thing was that he was actually addicted to milk. He often had an overwhelming desire to drink milk *even though he knew it made his colitis much worse.*

So far we have just been dowsing for yes and no answers. You may well have experienced different strengths of response, some being weaker than others. Obviously it is important to be able to distinguish between things that are of major importance and those of minor effect. Rather than rely on the strength of dowsing response, which particularly for beginners can vary from day to day, some form of more accurate response is helpful. What is needed is the simplest possible system that will give accurate results.

The use of a rule was mentioned in Chapter 4 (see p. 46). A metre rule is marked off in 100 units and is therefore not suitable for what we need. It is easier to use a shorter graduated line, and 20 centimetres is a suitable length. Taking a piece of paper or card, draw a line exactly 20 centimetres long on it. Mark off the line in centimetre increments and then mark the half-way point with the number 0. Mark each centimetre point to the right of this with numbers increasing by +1 each time, so that the most right-hand number will be +10. Repeat this process going left from the centre, but this time marking the points with a minus sign, the most left-hand point will now be −10. The final result will appear something like Figure 9. This will now be your measuring system. Put the item to be tested just above the 0 mark and a sample of your own hair just to the right of the 10 mark. The latter is not absolutely necessary as you are dowsing for yourself, but a small lock of hair will help to fix the idea of what you are dowsing for. The system is based on the concept that the nearer to the reading of +10 your response is, the better the food will be for you. Start dowsing from the −10 end of the scale, slowly moving up the scale towards the +10 end. Watch carefully for any change in the pendulum swing. All being well the pendulum will swing off into a maximum positive answer at some point along the scale. If it is below zero, then that food is definitely not for you. The further it is towards +10 the better for you it will be. Figure 10 shows just such a dowse being carried out.

If your dowsing leads you to suspect that you are allergic to particular foods, then why not take the risk and trust your dowsing? Try cutting those suspect foods out of your

	NEGATIVE										0			POSITIVE							
−10	−9	−8	−7	−6	−5	−4	−3	−2	−1			1	2	3	4	5	6	7	8	9	10

Figure 9. Dowsing with scale calibrated for both negative and positive values

Figure 10. Use of a hair sample when dowsing

diet for at least a fortnight and see how you get on. It won't hurt you, and you may well be surprised how much better you feel. Food allergies are common. However, before you become too involved, remember that it may be additives or sprayed crops that you are allergic to, rather than the basic food. Hence, always test apparently identical foods from different sources and see if you obtain the same results.

60

THE STRESS FACTOR

It is important always to bear in mind that things change. One's allergic threshold can change remarkably with the level of stress that one is under. I remember the person who introduced me to Arthur Coca's book on food allergies telling me about his experiences. Using the pulse test he had determined that he was allergic to all the cabbage family, wheat and chocolate. He cut these out of his diet, and the change in his appearance was amazing. He regained lost weight and looked far fitter. The following summer he went away on holiday, and after a week he realised that unwittingly he had been eating 'allergic' foods without any reaction. He assumed that he had outgrown the problem and eat everything put before him for the rest of his holiday. No problems at all. He then went back to work where he put himself under a great deal of stress, and a couple of days later all his allergic food symptoms came back. His allergic threshold was stress-sensitive. This seems to be so for all the food allergy cases that I have come across. For this reason it is vitally important that one's diet is checked carefully, and when under stress to keep off foods that fall into the allergic or doubtful category.

Unfortunately, human nature being what it is, it is when we are under stress that we tend to crave most for the things that are the worst for us. Symptoms of illnesses as severe as multiple sclerosis have arisen from no more serious a cause than food allergies. There have been many remarkable changes in health from doing nothing more than changing diet and avoiding allergic foods.

So, it may be vital to find out what foods you are sensitive to, and if possible to avoid them. Particularly it is *vital* to keep off allergic foods when ill, or under any other stress. Dowsing is an ideal method of checking for these sensitivities, particularly as it is then possible, for the majority of people, to check the results with the pulse test.

The importance of having a good diet cannot be stressed

too much. By good, I mean a diet that is right for you personally. For example, a high-fibre diet is now accepted as being necessary for good health, even in orthodox circles. But how do we get our fibre? Bran is often suggested as being one of the best sources of dietary fibre. By this, most people mean wheat bran. Unfortunately, an appreciable number of the population are allergic to wheat bran, so they may make their health worse by eating it. In such cases remember that there are many alternatives. For instance, oat bran (often sold with oatgerm) is a softer fibre, more palatable for most people, and weight for weight is more effective in the diet than wheat bran.

Unfortunately, until recently, the commonly accepted doctrine was that a 'normal' diet was perfectly adequate and that people who took things like vitamin supplements were cranks. Nothing could be further from the truth. I well remember a farmer talking to me about diet. 'When I have a sick beast and call the vet, he always asks me, "What have you been feeding it on?" When I am ill, my doctor never asks me what I have been eating!' We are more complex in many ways than other animals, so it is likely that we should be even more sensitive to diet than they are.

As a starting point to good health, look therefore at your diet. Dowsing for your food is not only interesting and good dowsing practice, but it may reveal things that can really change your health for the better in ways that no amount of medication can do.

Before you can check your diet with dowsing, you need first of all to have some idea of what comprises a good diet. Basically, we need to have an adequate intake of all the essential vitamins and minerals along with adequate protein, fat, carbohydrate and dietary fibre. The imbalances in these elements that occur in the 'normal' western diet will now be examined in the next chapter.

CHAPTER 6

DIET AND DIETARY SUPPLEMENTS

Dowsing can determine your correct balanced diet, including any additional vitamin and mineral supplements that are required. This application will have long-term beneficial effects on your health.

For many years now there have been a large number of people who have taken vitamins and minerals to supplement their diets. Orthodox medical opinion has generally been that such supplements are unnecessary. The commonly held view has been that a balanced diet will contain all that we need. Unfortunately, there is a growing weight of evidence to show that such ideas are complaisant to say the least.

Before looking into the relevant dowsing aspects, it is prudent and informative to have a brief look at the background to the problem. After all, in whatever field dowsing is used, it is foolish not to have an adequate background knowledge of the subject.

If it is required to know what, if any, vitamin and mineral supplements are needed, then it is necessary to know what constitutes a balanced diet. Unfortunately for some people who would like to think otherwise, corn flakes for breakfast, baked beans for lunch and fish and chips for tea is not a balanced diet. To know what balanced really means, we must look back into history, indeed into pre-history.

In spite of what the rapid rise of modern technology

might suggest, humankind has evolved slowly over the centuries. Our bodies and digestive systems are similar to those of people living many thousands of years ago. In those times there were no fast-food chains, only people running fast trying to catch their food! In the times before written history we can turn to the archaeologists to find out how our ancestors lived.

People lived primarily as hunters of animals and gatherers of vegetable foods. Considering the so-called primitive tribes that were discovered in this century, they all seem to have this pattern of living. Growing crops purposefully and domesticating animals has been a recent development in terms of our evolutionary time. This means that the individual's diet has changed enormously over the last ten thousand years or so, and this is a short time in terms of evolutionary change. Even more significantly, the vast majority of changes to our diets have occurred within the last two hundred years.

People as hunter-gatherers would have had variable diets, depending on climatic and other external conditions, and would have lived in the warmer parts of the world. Remember that the present climates are not the same that they once were — archaeologists show us that Britain, for instance, was once much warmer than it is now. The main diet would have therefore been vegetables (roots, stems, leaves and seeds), fruits, nuts and whatever animals could be caught, most likely also grubs and insects and, occasionally, honey from wild bees.

The vast majority of people no longer benefit from the exercise that our ancestors were used to. Neither is the diet of the majority of the civilised (i.e. town-dwelling) world like that of our ancestors. Biologically, both these factors must affect our well-being, as our bodies are designed more for a pre-history type of living.

In the area of diet, what are likely to be the major changes? Considering the convenience foods, there is a tendency for only a few ingredients to make up the major part of the food. These items are white wheat flour, saturated fats and white sugar. Of these, the fats are often synthetic (margarines), and the white flour includes chemical additives. These bear no resemblance at all to what our ancestors ate. They had no sugar, little fat, except animal fats and that in nuts and seeds, and no refined flour. The meat in wild animals contains far less fat than in our domesticated animals, and in that reduced amount of fat, a far higher amount was unsaturated. The type of flour obtained from grinding wild cereals contains more minerals, fibre and protein, and less starch, than our present heavily 'developed' cultivated cereals.

Our present average diet contains too little fibre, too few vitamins, too little minerals, too much sugar, too much fat and often too much starch. Also food often contains synthetic additives that the human body has never had to metabolise before this century. This is also a cause for concern.

In short, our diet — unless we are very different from the average person — will be unbalanced compared with what genetically our digestive system was developed for. It is instructive to dowse over a whole range of foods bearing all this in mind. Try dowsing over such things as sugar, white flour, butter, and margarine, to see if they are needed in your next meal. For the majority of people the answer will be no. If you normally eat a lot of sweet things and fatty things and obtain a yes answer, then I would suspect that your dowsing ability is being overridden by wishful thinking.

So what can be done? First of all a change in diet will be effective. Reduce the consumption of sugar, fats and refined flour to much lower levels. Cut down cultivated meat intake: most people eat far too much meat of whatever form. Eat more vegetables of all types. Then we will not need any vitamin or mineral supplements? Wrong!

Modern farming techniques, with its heavy dependence on chemical fertilisers affect the mineral, and sometimes vitamin content of the food grown. The overenthusiastic use of NPK fertilisers (Nitrogen Phosphorous Potassium) has seriously reduced the plant uptake of many minerals that are vital for our wellbeing. So even changing our diet to a more natural form will not necessarily give us all we need. Considerable additions to a diet may be needed unless food can be grown on healthy soil without deficiencies.

MINERAL REQUIREMENTS

Minerals are the simplest chemicals that may be needed additions to a diet, so let us look at them first. A good book should always be available as a reference, and I personally find that the one quoted below[13] is a mine of useful information.

Many minerals are basically metal compounds, the metal being the thing that the body needs. There are quite a number of these so-called trace elements. Iron is perhaps the best-known one, and an iron deficiency will cause anaemia, as the red blood corpuscles are based on iron. Unfortunately an iron deficiency cannot be remedied by swallowing iron powder. The body needs iron in a form that it has always absorbed from natural sources, not crude chemicals. I remember reading an article on iron absorbtion in *The New Scientist* which stated that iron sulphate was worse than useless and could even cause a bodily loss of iron. Yet even though that research was published some fifteen years ago, I believe the blood transfusion service still give away free iron (ferrous) sulphate tablets to blood donors. Ferrous fumarate and ferrous gluconate are absorbed more effectively by the body.

There is a long list of minerals that the body may need. Some supplement manufacturers produce tablets that are meant to give an adequate supply for all our needs — but do they?

Take the element selenium[13]. This element is concerned with longevity and the maintenance of the auto-immune system. It also helps reduce the risk of strokes or heart disease. People living in areas where long healthy lifespans are known, all have a large amount of selenium in their diets. Modern farming methods have caused the amount of selenium in our foodstuffs to drop by about 50 per cent in the last twenty years.

For a long lifespan we seem to need over 100 micrograms of organically combined selenium per day. The American Recommended Daily Allowance (RDA) is 125 micrograms, yet some mineral supplements contain only ten micrograms for a daily dose. Surprise, surprise, the British authorities have not even suggested an RDA. The same thing applies for many other minerals.

Taking into account that everyone will have a different diet *and a different mineral requirement* how do we set about deciding what we need? Again, dowsing provides an ideal solution as items can be decided on an individual basis, rather than on published figures or manufacturers' data. That way one can keep a check on one's progress and make sure that the amount taken is correct for one's needs at the time.

How should you get started? Firstly I would recommend getting a good book on vitamins and minerals so that you can check your dowsing results. You are unlikely to get into trouble from such supplements if your dowsing gives doses within a manufacturer's recommended figures, but it is always best to have some idea of what you are doing.

One excellent method of dowsing requires the buying of tablets of the whole range of minerals (and vitamins too if you are going to deal with them at the same time). First of all, assuming that you are using a pendulum, hold it over each bottle in turn with the mental question, 'Do I need this

13.   Erdman, Dr Robert, and Jones, Merion, *Minerals, The Metabolic Miracle Workers*, pp. 101–4, Century, 1988.

particular mineral in addition to my food?' This will sort out which ones are needed. Then take some tablets out of one of the 'yes' bottles and dowse over one of them to start with. 'Is this sufficient supplement?' can be the next question. If the answer is no, then add another tablet and dowse over the pair with the same question. Keep on adding tablets until a firm positive 'yes' is obtained. Then look at the recommended dose. Is your result less than that figure? If it is then all is well. If it is slightly above, then there should be no problem. If it is well above then read up on that particular mineral *carefully*. Your dowsing may be quite correct, but always remember that dowsing accuracy often takes time to develop.

How about the different manufacturers' minerals? Are they all as good as each other? The short answer is no. Some are more beneficial than others. Like the problem with iron, some mineral forms are more easily assimilated than others. You can always dowse over the bottles in the shop to see which ones give the strongest reaction and go for those.

At this point you may well be aghast at the idea of dowsing openly in a shop, and decide to drop the whole idea. There are ways of dowsing however that are not obvious to the casual onlooker, which I often use when I do not wish to draw attention to myself. All that is needed is a little ingenuity.

I use a key ring that has a small crystal ball in it. This is on a short chain. Holding my keys in my hand it just looks as if I am idly holding my car keys, whereas in fact I am dowsing with the ball as a small pendulum. Just glancing at the ball occasionally is quite enough; the main thing is not to draw attention to the fact that you are interested in its movements. That way you can check before you buy, and maybe save yourself a lot of money in the process.

Of the minerals, I find that I use calcium, magnesium, iron, zinc and selenium the most frequently. Supplements like chromium I use rarely. Remember that different parts of the country have different mineral distributions, so that your requirements may well be different to mine.

So far we have been considering minerals. How about vitamins? Vitamins were first thought to be vital amines (nitrogen compounds) that were necessary for correct bodily function. That is where the name first came from. Nowadays the list includes many non-amine compounds like vitamin C, but the name has stuck. Basically vitamins are chemicals that are necessary for bodily life. Whereas minerals are simple chemical substances where the chemical form of the required element can be associated with different compounds, vitamins are quite specific and often complicated compounds. None of them, except vitamin B12 which contains cobalt, has any metal in its construction. They are compounds of carbon, oxygen, hydrogen and often nitrogen.

Just to confuse matters, some of them, like folic acid, are sometimes classed as being in the B group of vitamins, even though they have not been given a B number. Inadequate amounts of any vitamin will cause problems to bodily health. But what is the minimum amount needed?

It is here that we enter the minefield. Different authorities quote different amounts, and it is difficult to know what the true minimum figures are. For the Recommended Daily Allowance (RDA) of any particular vitamin it is not unusual to find that the American figures are greater than the British figures, where a British value is given. This cannot be due to anything else except different interpretations of research data, the people in the USA are not basically different to those in the UK.

Sometimes, like in the case of vitamin C, the RDA may be based on dubious information. The British RDA is based on the amount to prevent scurvy — in other words the assumption is that vitamin C is only of use in preventing scurvy. Yet vitamin C is now well known to have a host of valuable functions, including assisting the auto-immune system. Indeed in large dose rates it can assist in removing hardening (atheroma) from the arterial walls. The human being is one of few animals that cannot synthesise vitamin C within the body. If we look at the vitamin-C intake (or the vitamin-C level in the blood) of apes and other animals, to get the same level in human blood we would need about 4 grams of vitamin C per day, yet the RDA is only about one eightieth of that figure.

It follows that the official RDA figures for some vitamins are suspect. On the other hand, some vitamins are toxic in too large quantities, particularly vitamins A and D. So again we need to be cautious in our approach to adding vitamins to the diet. I can recommend keeping a good book on the subject to hand so that the results can be checked against a reliable reference[14].

Which vitamins are most likely to be needed? The most common deficiencies that I come across are vitamins B, C and E. In particular vitamin C appears to be a key factor in activating many other vitamins and minerals in the body. Vitamins in the B group present a rather more complicated problem. Many of them are interdependent, so vitamin B6, for instance, should not normally be given in isolation. One safe way is to use tablets of the whole B complex, otherwise it means having stocks of all the separate compounds, and there are quite a few of them. You must also bear in mind that some of the vitamins need adequate mineral levels in the diet for them to be effective, so it is necessary to check both vitamins and minerals.

It is possible to dowse for vitamins item by item, but, as has just been mentioned, there are quite a lot of them. The simpler way for the beginner is to start with vitamins A, B complex, C, D and E. All one then needs to do is to dowse for the number of tablets to take per day at mealtimes. This is not the most exact method, but it will give good results in most cases.

---

14. Mervyn, L., *Thorsons Complete Guide to Vitamins and Minerals*, Thorsons, 1986.

You can go into a health food shop and dowse over their stock of mineral and vitamin supplements. I have done this in the past, and it has saved me from buying unsuitable tablets.

What, you may ask, are unsuitable tablets? Without trying to be clever, the answer is those that do not suit you! For instance vitamin-C tablets are nearly always made from synthetic vitamin C, i.e. not derived from plants. As vitamin C (ascorbic acid) is a simple chemical, this will most likely be perfectly acceptable to your body, just like the natural chemical. However, some vitamin-C tablets contain 'bioflavonoids' derived from plants. These are meant to assist the utilisation of the vitamin C by the body. On one occasion I obtained a strong negative response from a particular make of vitamin-C tablet. Cheap synthetic vitamin-C powder from Boots, OK — expensive 'better' vitamin C definitely not OK! I was puzzled until I realised that it was probably one of the bioflavonoids that I was allergic to. That indeed was the problem, as it turned out. I was allergic to the rose-hip that they put in the tablets.

So don't be surprised if you find that you experience different responses to different manufacturers' products. Trust your dowsing rather than the manufacturer's hype as more expensive is not necessarily better. Remember also that many vitamins are not natural products, they are synthesised in chemical processes. The biological activity of such chemically produced vitamins may be considerably less than their natural counterparts. Tests on rats have shown that the effectiveness of some synthetic vitamins was only about a third that of the natural product.

I recall vividly a friend of mine who started selling vitamins in one of the pyramid systems. She was enthusiastic about her products and tried to sell me some. They were pretty expensive. I looked at their advertising blurb which said how good the products were, and I asked her, 'Are the vitamins from natural sources?' She didn't know, but said that she would find out. To cut a long story short, all she could get out of her suppliers was that 'They bought from the best sources.' They refused to say which, if any, of their vitamins came from natural sources, merely repeating that they bought the best available.

Now I appreciate that the borderline between synthetic and natural is thin at times, but what made me cross was their inference that their products were natural, this not being directly stated, but inferred. No court of law would have convicted them on misrepresentation, but like a lot of advertising it went right to the edge of legality.

So here is an ideal place to practise your dowsing, because the information that you find will be difficult to obtain in any other way. I am including in Appendix 2 (see p. 175) tables of the most common minerals, vitamins and other elements that are necessary in the diet. The official recommended daily allowance and the commonly accepted, more realistic, daily allowance figures are also included. Where there can be toxic effects from large doses, these are mentioned too.

Incidentally, it is worth remembering that not all the factors in food that are vital to good health may yet have been discovered. It is all too easy to think that, providing all the known minerals, vitamins, fibre, protein, etc., are present, your diet will be satisfactory. This makes the dangerous assumption that we know everything about diet and that nothing remains to be discovered.

I once attended a lecture at one of the 'Health and Healing' conferences run by the Wrekin Trust. This was given by a Canadian specialist on dietary matters. He quoted the ingredients of a tomato sauce for use on pizzas: all the thirty-odd ingredients were synthetic. More worrying was what we were told about a brand of synthetic egg yolk. Apparently at that time, about ten years ago, there was a glut of egg-white in Canada at the egg processing plants. Someone had the idea of making a dry synthetic egg yolk that could be packed up with the dried egg-white. The combination was sold as a dried egg substitute for use in cooking. At a Canadian university they did some tests on this product.

Now raw eggs are a good diet for rats; they can live well on nothing else. So they did a controlled experiment. One group of rats was fed on raw eggs, the others were fed on reconstituted Eggo, or whatever it was called. We were shown a photograph of a specimen rat from each group after a fortnight. The raw egg rat was a beautiful fit and healthy specimen, the other looked appalling: wizened, ill and old. The experiment was to have run for six weeks, but they terminated it after three. All the artificial-egg rats were dead.

Bearing in mind that the artificial egg yolks were meant to reproduce exactly the constituents in raw egg yolk: proteins, vitamins, minerals, etc., then one is right to be concerned. In terms of food quality the artificial yolk fell far short of the natural counterpart. This is the unacceptable technology gap between what we think should happen and what actually does.

So check over your foods and those on the supermarket shelves. See if your dowsing shows up recurrent 'no' reactions for particular additives. Check over 'fresh' food-stuffs like fruit and vegetables. Maybe they are tainted with sprays of various sorts. Perhaps, as I suspect in the case of some imported strawberries, they are irradiated for longer life (the strawberries life, not yours!) Above all, providing that your results are not obviously suspect, start to trust your dowsing. Providing that your results do not unnecessarily restrict your diet, in which case you may well be trying too hard, then it should have a beneficial effect on your health.

CHAPTER 7

DOWSING FOR
MEDICINES

*This chapter considers the use of dowsing for determining
appropriate remedies, particularly in the field of complementary
medicine. Biochemic remedies (tissue salts) are used as the
starting point, as they are a suitable, effective and safe way of
entering into dowsing for medicines.*

So far we have been concerning ourselves with changing
our diet as a means to better health. This is fine providing
that the body is sufficiently well to be able to respond to
these methods of treatment, but what happens when something is needed more than the changes that an improved
diet can bring?

Once the field of medicines and other therapies is entered, there is a completely new field to be considered. For a
start, the range of possible therapies is immense. Secondly,
some of the therapeutic areas are very much within the
province of orthodox medical practice.

If one is to make sense of the therapeutic area, then, as
previously, it is best to go slowly. It is too easy to get carried
away with enthusiastic ideas and to lose track of reality. So
first of all, let us have a look at just what is meant by illness
and disease.

Firstly, we need to distinguish between acute, temporary
and chronic illnesses. Acute illnesses are those where life
may well be threatened in the immediate future. Often
these are the areas that are best left to conventional medi-

74

cine and orthodox treatment. This is the philosophy adopted in much of modern China and it seems to work well there. Acute illnesses, like severe bacterial infections or internal problems needing immediate surgery, are not normally suitable areas for purely complementary techniques. This is not to say that alternative methods of treatment cannot be used at the same time, but in general complementary methods of treatment work more slowly than, for instance, antibiotics. In life-threatening situations one cannot afford to hang about.

Temporary illness I am defining as illnesses where the body's defence systems will overcome the problem, given time. In this case methods of treatment are needed that will work in harmony with the body to speed up recovery. Often this is quite easy to achieve.

In the third category, chronic illness, usually a much more difficult problem is being faced. Here a situation is being considered where, for whatever reason, the body has developed into a 'locked' state where it is unable to break free from the illness. This is the area where conventional medicine can do little for the patient but alleviate symptoms, and often there is steady degeneration of the health of the patient. For such cases keys are needed that will unlock the system so that recovery becomes possible. In all illness, remember that ultimately it is the body's own systems that produce recovery; what we do with our therapies is give it a helping hand.

In China, both western and traditional Chinese medicines are practised side-by-side. The latter is a blend of herbal and acupuncture treatment. The Chinese attitude is that acute illness that will respond to western medicine should be treated that way as it is usually more effective. Other classes of illness tend to be treated with the traditional methods, as these have often been shown to work where western medicine is ineffective.

Dowsing can be used for both orthodox and complementary methods of treatment. Indeed some orthodox medical

75

practitioners use dowsing methods in their practice, but this is unusual. For this reason the emphasis will be on complementary methods of treatment, as these will be the ones that are open to the majority of readers. However, the methods outlined can be used within orthodox medical practice just as easily.

Let us therefore start by looking at mild, or slow-acting chronic illnesses. Here there is no urgency, and therefore no emotional pressure that could otherwise affect the accuracy of one's dowsing.

COMPLEMENTARY MEDICINE

If you are new to the subject of complementary medicine, and have no developed skills in this area, then you need to try treatment methods that can be easily checked, and where, if a mistake is made, nothing disastrous will happen. For this reason I suggest that the Schuessler Biochemic Remedies (Tissue Salts) are used as a starting point. They also have the advantage of being readily available through most health-food shops. I began with these when I branched out into the treatment of illness, and found them extremely helpful. They are based on the chemical compounds that remain after a body has been cremated, these being the major minerals present in the body. The compounds are based on sodium, potassium, calcium, iron, magnesium and silica. In turn these are combined with several acid bases, chloride, sulphate, phosphate and fluoride. In all, Dr Schuessler ended up with twelve compounds that he felt were essential to bodily health. A photograph of a few of these medicines, as packaged commercially, is shown in Figure 11.

This method of treatment might seem to be perfectly acceptable to orthodox medicine, except for one factor. The strength of the compounds is small. They are diluted down, in a carrier of milk sugar, to a concentration of only one part

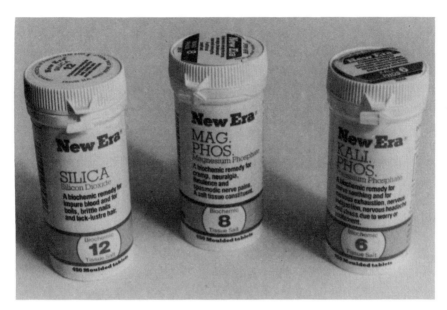

Figure 11. Three of the biochemic remedies

in one million. In other words they are at a low level of homoeopathic potency. Orthodox theories would lead one to expect that such small concentrations could have no effect on the human body, yet I know from my own experience that they can work effectively.

At this point I would like to leave any discussion of the possible mechanisms of operation until later on, in the section on homoeopathic medicines (see pp. 84–98). All that is necessary now is to take their validity on trust.

Because of their low concentration of active principles, one can take much more than the recommended dose of the biochemic remedies without any risk to health whatever. They are therefore an appropriate subject to start off with for our dowsing. The Biochemic Handbook that goes with the remedies[15] gives a lot of detail about which remedies

---

15.   Chapman, J.B., MD, *Dr Schuessler's Biochemistry*, New Era Laboratories Ltd., Cecil House, Holborn Viaduct, London EC1.

one should use for specific ailments. However, for our purposes it is best to dowse first, and then check in the book to see what it says.

I find that about 80 per cent of the time I obtain results that are in agreement with the book. Twenty per cent of the time I obtain different results. By long experience I know that my dowsing produces better results than relying on the book. Why should this be so? I think that it is because dowsing can get to the root of what treatment is *needed* at a particular time. Prescribing from an analysis of obvious symptoms is not always the best way because there may well be symptoms that have not been noticed. *These less obvious symptoms may be the most important.* This is acknowledged in traditional Chinese acupuncture where many different aspects of the body are examined, not just the well-known multiple pulse tests.

In the final outcome it is the end result of the treatment that matters. I remember the time when my two sons were small and couldn't get to sleep at night. If I gave them the remedy that came up by dowsing (often Mag. Phos. — Magnesium Phosphate), they would drop off to sleep in just a few minutes. Also, if in the morning they claimed to be too ill to go to school, I would dowse to see if that was actually so. Often they were just trying to get a day off school. In those cases I dowsed for which biochemic remedy would help them, gave them the tablets and said they would now be perfectly OK. Grudgingly, they would then go off to school, knowing they had been rumbled yet having no effective method of countering it. It saved an awful lot of arguments at that time.

So how does one dowse for the remedies? Keep in mind that you may well be dowsing for somebody else. A system is therefore needed that is more universal than one that is only suitable for dowsing for ourselves.

The rule concept can again be used. In this case, however, a 'witness' (i.e. sample) is needed which represents the patient. This can be a lock of hair, a blood-spot on a piece of clean blotting paper, or a urine sample. Other things like nail clippings have been used. The rule only need give us 'yes' or 'no' answers in the first instance, but you will need to know the dose rate later. For this reason I suggest that you use a scale divided into ten equal divisions as shown in Figure 12. The witness is put on the right-hand side of the scale, and the medicine to be tested on the left-hand side. The pendulum is then used to determine the point where maximum reaction is obtained.

If the pendulum gives a maximum reaction about the zero point on the scale, then the medicine is not needed. Readings of less than 3 normally mean that little effect will be obtained and that the medicine is of little value at that time. Readings greater than 5 indicate that the medicine will be of considerable help. The nearer the reading is to 10, the greater the effect the remedy will be expected to have.

An easy way of checking all twelve remedies is now available. All that is required is to check them one at a time and note down all readings greater than 3. In general terms, it is unwise to give more than three different remedies at a time. It is better to start with the ones giving maximum responses and then to recheck the medicines, say a day later. Don't be surprised if you only get one medicine, but even so always check after a day or two to see if things have changed. If the medicine is affecting the body's defence systems, then the required treatment can change quite rapidly.

So far, so good. But how about the dose rate? The containers will have a recommended dose marked on them, but this will probably not be the optimum. Orthodox drugs affect people in greatly differing amounts, and homoeopathic medicines are no different. The individual's sensi-

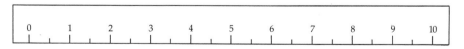

Figure 12. Dowsing scale calibrated 0–10

tivity varies depending on body chemistry and state of health. What is needed is a method for establishing how many tablets to take at a time, and how often they should be taken.

A scale has been used to dowse for the remedies to use, so why not use the same system for the number of tablets and the number of times they have to be taken? The answer is that the same system *can* be used; it is not necessary to use a completely different method for the changed circumstances. In the past dowsers used all sorts of fancy systems with calibrated triangles and other methods, in fact anything to make it look as if a new system was being used for the new type of answers required. These complex methods arose from a belief that dowsing for different properties needed a different method for each property to be dowsed for. Admittedly such complicated systems may help to keep things separate from a logical point of view, but in fact they are quite unnecessary.

So far, a scale has been used between a sample from the patient and the medicine, looking for a point of maximum reaction between them. This has been said to operate because of an affinity between the medicine and the patient's witness. The problem is that this is just not true. Dowsing has no respect for cosy theories, and this must always be remembered. What matters is whether methods work; how they work is a different matter altogether. Unfortunately far too many people, including dowsers, feel that if a phenomenon exists, then it must be explicable in terms that they can comprehend. It is at the point that we have got to that logical explanations begin to fall.

Replace the scale by another one calibrated 0 to 10, but marked under or on top in large capitals NUMBER OF TABLETS PER DOSE (see Fig. 13). Now try dowsing again, using a medicine that gave a strong positive reaction as the witness, *this time for the size of dose.* All being well a different balance point will be located on the scale from the one previously obtained for that medicine. For the biochemic

Figure 13. Dowsing scale for the size of dose

remedies, one would expect an answer between, say, 1 and 5 for the number of tablets to be taken at a time.

Replace the scale with another one marked NUMBER OF DOSES PER DAY (see Fig. 14), and redowse using the same medicine witness. All the information that is needed for that particular medicine should now be available. The process can then be repeated for any other medicine that was indicated.

This is basically how to dowse for the biochemic remedies: first for the remedy, secondly for the size of dose, and thirdly for the number of doses per day. The only factor that has changed has been the inscription on the scale. If the exercise is now repeated with a bare scale with no inscription, but concentrating mentally on the question, 'Will this remedy help the person represented by the witness, answers between 0 and 10, please?' then the same answers should be obtained as in the original dowsing. Next, taking one of the indicated medicines, focus on the thought, 'What size of dose in tablets does this person need?' and dowse for the answer. Finally, change the question to, 'How many doses per day does the patient need?'

Exactly the same answers should be obtained whether a plain scale is used or one with inscriptions marked on it, however it may be helpful at the beginning to use different scales for the three different solutions to the problem being

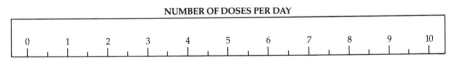

Figure 14. Dowsing scale for the dose rate

81

dowsed for. Reminding yourself of the object of your dowsing can help accuracy. Nevertheless in the final analysis a simple bare scale and different mental questions is all that is needed.

In other words *it is the question in your mind that matters*. This was mentioned earlier, but it is important to remember this factor. This method of dowsing is the one called 'question and answer'. What matters is that the question is clearly stated *and is unambiguous*.

At this point I would not be in the least surprised if many readers felt that the whole process was becoming unbelievable. So too did I in my early days of dowsing; it all seemed too far fetched. Remember that you are not working with the logical side of the brain, except in interpreting the information that is obtained. The information is coming from the intuitive side (see pp. 135–8). Providing that care is taken in setting up the rules that are being worked to, then your dowsing will accommodate those rules, strange though it may seem.

This last point, clearly setting up the rules, once tripped me up when dowsing for a patient. I was dowsing for how many drops of a particular medicine should be taken at a time. I obtained a slight response on three drops, a slight response on four drops and nothing else. I repeated the process and found exactly the same results. This was strange to say the least, as I had obtained a very positive reaction from the medicine itself. Finally, getting nowhere fast, I dowsed for three and a half drops — and obtained a very positive answer!

How on earth does one get half a drop? I tried dowsing for seven drops of half-strength medicine — '*No!*' Finally, in desperation I dowsed for, 'Am I asking a silly question?' and obtained a definite positive answer! After quite a few abortive tests, I finally found the answer — the medicine was not to be taken at a fixed dose rate. If I remember correctly it had to be taken at a high dose to start, and with reducing concentration of dose in the following days. I finished up by

82

giving the client a chart for the next fortnight's doses. This demonstrated clearly to me the necessity of leaving a route open so that an incorrect assumption can be detected. As mentioned earlier, I do this nowadays by having 'yes-but' and 'no-but' dowsing responses available.

The Schuessler Tissue Salts are therefore a suitable, and a safe way of entering into dowsing for medicines. My experience has been that they can be helpful at times. These salts are at a low concentration of one part in one million, and therefore absolutely safe. There is, however, a problem. How can it be that a concentration of only one part in a million of a simple salt such as Nat Mur (sodium chloride or common salt) can have healing properties when millions of times this dose of salt may be used on a plate of fish-and-chips? If one biochemic tablet can give help, salted fish-and-chips should help far more.

In some ways there is a common problem in dowsing and homoeopathic type medicines: logic suggests that neither of them should work, yet practical experience shows that they do work, and usually, in skilled hands, they work very well indeed.

It is therefore time to look further into the whole area of homoeopathy and homoeopathic treatment. This class of medical treatment is suitable for the dowser to work with, as the results are easily checked. Also for the beginner it has the advantage, like the biochemic remedies, that it is highly unlikely any harm will be caused to a patient if an incorrect remedy is prescribed.

CHAPTER 8
HOMOEOPATHIC REMEDIES

How homoeopathic remedies may work, and their advantages are described, as well as methods for determining the correct remedies to use, and their administration. The number of homoeopathic medicines available is extremely large, and dowsing can offer a practical solution to cost cutting, to selection of the remedy, and its correct potency.

Homoeopathic medicines can be used by the lay person perfectly well, particularly for first-aid situations. With dowsing skills, the field of application in homoeopathic medicines opens much wider still. They are much more powerful than the biochemic remedies when dealing with deep-rooted problems, but often they need to be used with counselling skills at the same time. Whenever dealing with illness that is rooted deep in a person's emotional history, there is often the necessity to be able to give support and guidance at a personal level.

So what are homoeopathic medicines, and how do they work? To answer this, it is appropriate to look into the origins of homoeopathy and see how it all started.

Early last century a certain Dr Samuel Hahnemann was exploring the treatment of serious illness by the use of toxic materials. This form of treatment had recently become popular and was giving considerable success in difficult cases. For instance mercury was being used to treat syphilis. The problem, mirrored in the side-effects of modern drugs, was that in many cases the treatment caused nearly as much distress as the illness, and sometimes more so. Hahnemann decided to see what happened if he reduced the dose of these highly toxic materials. If with a reducing dose the toxic effects reduced faster than the therapeutic effect, then he felt that it might be possible to treat the majority of cases with less toxicity. If that was the case, then he would be able to help patients without the severe toxic effects on the patient's system, which, in turn, acted against the therapeutic effect of the medicine.

He therefore carried out a whole series of tests, and discovered that his assumption was correct. In fact, the toxicity reduced much more rapidly than the therapeutic effect. He suddenly realised that he was getting good therapeutic effects with dilutions that were less than one hundredth of the accepted dose. In true scientific spirit he therefore decided to see at just what level of dilution the therapeutic effects stopped. He kept on diluting his medicines further and further, but still they worked. Indeed their effect seemed to get stronger the further the dilution progressed. Finally he was working with medicines that contained less than one million millionth part of active material — and still they worked.

This is the basis of the homoeopathic dose. The fact that there may be no convenient explanation is irrelevant. Like dowsing, the justification has to be that it works. The lack of a current accepted scientific theory to explain it, does not mean that it cannot work.

The toxic therapies that Hahnemann started his work from were noted to give symptoms in a healthy patient that were just about identical to those shown by the illness that was being treated. In other words mercury poisoning shows similar effects to a syphilis infection; strychnine gives the same symptoms as lockjaw (tetanus), and so on. This 'like cures like' had been observed before Hahnemann discovered that only small doses were necessary for treatment. The like-cures-like concept is now the standard method of proving new homoeopathic medicines. Determine the symptoms of a large dose of a prospective treatment compound on a healthy patient, and those will be the symptoms in an ill patient that the medicine will emulate, thus stimulating an appropriate response from the body's auto-immune system.

Homoeopathic means 'like pathology' or 'like symptoms', and describes the method by which the system of treatment arose. The real breakthrough of Hahnemann was in discovering that a very small dose is all that is needed. The concentrations still use the old Latin names such as 6X or 10C, where X means 10 and C means 100. Hence 6X means 10 raised to the power of 6, i.e. $10 \times 10 \times 10 \times 10 \times 10 \times 10$ which equals one million. In other words a 6X dilution means one part in one million of the original substance is all that is left. 10C means ten hundreds multiplied together, or that one hundred, million, million, millionth part of the original material is all that is present. Maybe less than one atom of the original material is in a tablet of the medicine.

How can it possibly work? Perhaps it is due to the method of preparation. For instance a 4C dilution is made as follows. One part of the original substance is dissolved in one hundred parts of water, and the whole is firmly shaken together ('succussed'). This is 1C dilution. One part of this is mixed with one hundred parts of water and succussed. This is 2C dilution. One part of this is taken and succussed with 100 parts of water. This is 3C dilution. Finally one part of this is mixed with 100 parts of water and succussed to form the final 4C medicine.

One theory is that the molecular imprint of the original material is impressed on the water, and this replicates down through the successive dilutions. Maybe so. Water is a sensitive and rather anomalous material; it could happen but other people have different theories. Ultimately all that matters is that homoeopathic medicine works. In the UK it is often not realised that on the continent of Europe about half of all medicines prescribed are homoeopathic.

There is one basic problem with homoeopathic medicines that has nothing to do with their effectiveness, and that is the lack of patent protection. Anyone can set up to manufacture homoeopathic medicines if they so wish, providing that they meet the requirements of the manufacturing processes. Automatically, this means that no-one can make large profits out of homoeopathic medicine manufacture as any that were excessively expensive would soon be undercut by another manufacturer's products. Indeed, this is the case with homoeopathic medicines at present. They are inexpensive to produce and are sold with very modest 'mark-ups'. Having inexpensive medicines might be thought of as an advantage, but it is only an advantage to the consumer.

I once tried to interest a large retailer in an electronic design of mine. I told him how it would be cheaper than competitive products. He was not interested unless he had a mark-up greater than his existing lines. In other words if he made £10 profit on his existing products he would only consider mine if he made at least £10 on them! He was not really concerned with selling price. His argument was as follows.

'These are not impulse-buy articles, so I only sell them to people who want them. A reduced price will only marginally increase sales, so if your product is half the present price, with the same percentage mark-up as my present line, I will make only just over half the profit that I do at present. To be safe, I need to be able to make the same actual, not percentage, mark-up as I do at the moment.'

The same argument can be applied to medicines. They have a relatively fixed volume market. Low-cost medicines, if at fixed percentage mark-ups, would not be welcomed by pharmaceutical retailers if they replaced existing expensive products. Perhaps this is one reason why homoeopathic medicines are not actively promoted in this country.

The patient, of course, views it rather differently. The medicines are inexpensive, non-tasting, non-toxic and normally have few side-effects. I would not suggest that homoeopathic medicines can be used successfully in all cases of disease and illness, but there is no doubt that accurately prescribed they can be used for the vast majority of purposes that are treated by more expensive drugs. The absence of serious side-effects is also important. Many hospital cases are there because the person is suffering from 'Iatrogenic Illness'. This is a cover-up-phrase which really means that the patient is suffering from the effects of their previous treatment, normally drugs. All that is needed is a glance at the horrendously high figures for medically induced drug-addiction in this country form the benzo-diaze-pines (antidepressants such as ativan, valium and librium, and sleeping tablets such as mogadon) to realise that the non-addictive homoeopathic approach is long overdue in this country.

Assuming that you wish to try using homoeopathic medicines, how does dowsing fit into the picture? Will it work, and if so is it better than conventional methods of prescribing?

The first thing to consider is the range of homoeopathic medicines available. It is extremely large. There are several *thousand* homoeopathic medicines to choose from. This has always been a problem with homoeopathy. The wide range is necessary to cover all the small nuances in symptom patterns. For instance, if suffering from a cold, then classical homoeopathic prescribing means that all facets of the person's symptoms need to be considered. These will include stuffed-up or runny nose, blocked sinuses, skin colour, temperature, sweating, etc., etc. This all takes a considerable time, and even then the practitioner may well be faced with several possible alternative medicines. In general terms, in homoeopathy a prescription for an incorrect medicine will have little or no effect. Hence it is sometimes necessary to try several alternatives if the first one is not effective, or only partially so. The skill and experience of the practitioner makes all the difference; much more fine-tuning is necessary than with conventional drug therapy. In homoeopathy one is treating the whole patient, not just the main obvious symptom.

Suppose the most suitable medicine has been found, then what? A whole range of potencies is available from 6X up to 100C and beyond. How is the correct potency and dose rate chosen? Will another medicine be needed as a follow up? All these factors show why homoeopathic medicine has needed to be approached from a long period of study and training.

Because the effects of homoeopathic medicines become stronger with increased dilution, the high potencies are those with the highest dilutions. Also it must be remembered that high potencies can have large sudden effects, whatever type of medicine is used. Hence 6X (low) potency medicines work slowly but are unlikely to cause any problems. High potencies sometimes only need a single dose, but they can cause trauma to the body — even severe shock.

I mentioned in the introduction that it was homoeopathic medicine that got me back on my feet after Asian Flu. It was the late Dr Westlake who prescribed the medicine for me, and he did all the analysis for the treatment by dowsing from a blood-spot that I sent to him through the post. It was about six years later before I had the pleasure of meeting him face-to-face.

For my 'flu he sent me two powders of high potency, and a bottle of tablets of homoeopathic phosphorous at much lower potency. I think that the high-potency powders were extract of thymus gland. He warned me that I might feel worse before I felt better, and it was just as well that he did. I had felt pretty dreadful before, but the effect of the powders was to make me feel suicidal — I knew that a complete breakdown was only a hair's breadth away. Somehow I hung on for a week, and then the tide turned. Within a fortnight I was feeling better than I had done for months. It took nearly a year for me to recover fully. I now realise that that is a short time for ME. Indeed without the treatment I am sure that I would have had a complete nervous breakdown with extremely serious consequences.

The effect of temporary aggravation of symptoms is a classical 'side-effect' of homoeopathic medicine. It is always a positive sign as it indicates that the correct remedy has been chosen and is stimulating the defences of the body. Too severe a reaction shows that the potency is rather too high for that particular patient. Patients vary in their sensitivity to treatment methods, and sensitive people tend to need considerably lower potencies for the same therapeutic effect.

It now is becoming obvious that homoeopathy is not an easy discipline for the beginner. There is a wide range of possible medicines combined with a wide range of potencies. For these reasons, in the past there have been few homoeopaths who have not had a long arduous training. Incidentally for medical practitioners in this country who wish to practise homoeopathy, it is a two-year full-time course *in addition to their normal medical training*. Small wonder therefore that few doctors practise homoeopathy. Dowsing however can give a different way into the subject, and again it is possible to check one's dowsing against the book to see if it makes sense.

Using dowsing, it is no longer necessary to remember long lists of remedies and their related symptoms. In dowsing one is merely looking for a resonance between the patient and a suitable medicine. Assuming that you can dowse competently, then you will have eliminated the need for a lot of book learning. There is one serious problem however, in its place you need to have samples of several thousand medicines. Suppose the correct medicine has been located after dowsing through 1500 medicines, and it takes ten seconds to dowse for each one, that is 15 000 seconds — over four hours to obtain the correct medicine. There is no way that one could work like this and some sort of short-cut is vital to make the system practical.

I have already described how dowsing is under mental control, and you can set up the rules yourself, so long as you are careful. Suppose a stock is kept of medicines packed

90

in boxes of 100 different remedies, ten rows by ten columns deep. Suppose there are twenty boxes. One could dowse over each box at a time asking, 'Is there a suitable remedy for the patient in this box?' A 'yes' answer means that only 100 remedies need to be checked through. Much more sensible.

The rules could be changed again. Taking the box containing the correct remedy, dowse for the row and column which contains the correct remedy (see Fig. 15). The point of intersection will be the correct one. Even if the remedy was in the twentieth box and the last row and last column of that box, you would only have had to dowse for 20 + 10 + 10 possibilities, i.e. forty times, and this is far better than 2000. The average dowsing time would be (at ten seconds per dowse) about three minutes per medicine. Perfectly acceptable. This is the method that I use when I have stocks of all the remedies that I wish to dowse over.

Next it is necessary to look up the medicine that has been selected in a suitable reference book[16] to see if it bears any resemblance to what is being looked for. If not, and if answers are found that do not make sense, then it is probably the dowsing technique that is at fault. Remember that there is no such thing as the universal dowser: just because you are good in one area of dowsing does not necessarily mean that you will be as successful in all the others. However, let us assume that the results are reasonable and appear to be correct. More information is needed before a satisfactory prescription can be made.

How about potencies? Firstly, in dowsing for a suitable medicine we were only looking for the best remedy, the potency was not mentioned. Suppose that a whole range of potencies of the medicine is available, then it is possible to dowse for the correct one. Suppose that a range of ten

---

16. Allen, H.C., *Keynotes of Leading Remedies*, Thorsens, 1985, or Kent, J.T., *Lectures on Homoeopathic Materia Medica with New Remedies*, Jain Publishing Co., New Delhi, 1982.

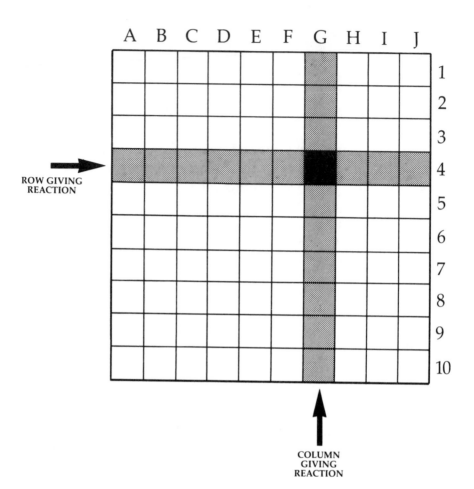

Figure 15. Location of a remedy by dowsing down rows and columns. The box contains 100 remedies (ten compartments wide and ten compartments deep). The correct remedy for this example will be in compartment G4 (seven columns along and four rows down)

potencies of each of the 2000 remedies is available. This means that 20 000 samples and the space for them will be needed. Conventional prescribing is now looking very attractive again.

All is not yet lost however. Suppose a scale is constructed, this time marked in equal increments, the units being of C potency. (It is not necessary to use the X potencies as 3C is the same as 6X). Mark the points on the rule as 0, 3, 5, 10,

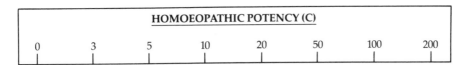

Figure 16. Scale for determining homoeopathic potency

20, 50, 100 and 200C. Put the sample at the zero mark and the patient's witness at the other end of the scale and dowse for the point of maximum reaction (see Fig. 16). If it is between calibrations, then the intermediate potency can be estimated. This way the correct potency can be determined without the need for large stocks of the different potencies.

The scale mentioned above does not use equal intervals between graduations. This may appear strange to anyone who is not used to graphs that have non-linear graduations. The reason is quite simple: homoeopathic potencies cover such an extremely wide range that a linear scale would make the low potencies, like 3C, nearly invisible on a linear scale going up to 200C.

Finally the correct dose rate and number of doses can be dowsed for as was done for the biochemic remedies. All that remains is to order the medicine from one of the homoeopathic medicine suppliers such as Ainsworths or Nelsons (addresses given at the end of the book, see p. 174).

CUTTING THE COST

A serious problem still remains. Several thousand remedies cost a lot of money and take up quite a lot of space. The cost will be the most prohibitive factor for most people and would certainly be in the order of thousands of pounds. This will deter most people from starting off, particularly if they thought that their dowsing was of doubtful accuracy at that time.

At this point, to find a solution to the problem of cost we need to go deeper into one of the more esoteric aspects of dowsing, that of dowsing from a list of remedies.

The first time that I came across the idea of dowsing from a list of things to determine which one was required, I was sceptical to say the least. Then I remembered that I originally felt the same way about dowsing itself. So I tried it out, and much to my surprise it worked. This is, I suppose, the parting of the ways. Whatever kind of theory one has previously looked for to explain dowsing — like radiation links between the medicine and the witness — falls to the ground at this point; there is, as far as I know, no adequate theory whatever to describe what happens in dowsing from an index or list of medicines. Yet from my own, and many others' experience, it works, uncomfortable though this may be to the rational mind, which regards this as the unacceptable face of dowsing. There would appear to be no rational explanation for such an idea. As described in the introduction, such a view is not scientific and ultimately what matters are the facts. Explanations can only come when our view of the universe is wide enough to be able to encompass them. In this case we are dealing with right-brain phenomena, so we need not be surprised that the logical left brain finds them uncomfortable. As the saying goes, 'Tough!'

The idea of dowsing down a list is not restricted to medicines. As one's skills develop, it is possible to use such ideas in other fields. I was once in Florence with the late Major Bruce McManaway. We were there to run a course on healing, and I was aware of my limited ability with the Italian language. One lunch time we went out to a local bar which served food. We had been told that the cooking was good traditional Italian, and that it was almost entirely frequented by the locals. That proved to be all too true. No-one there spoke English, and even the best Italian-speaking members of our party could not interpret more than about half of the menu. Someone jokingly said to me, 'Arthur, you have been showing us how to dowse from lists of things, how about choosing that way from the menu.' I realised that I had little option but to have a go. Muttering things about medicines not being the same as Italian menus, I took out my pendulum and dowsed down the incomprehensible list. One particular item gave a strong reaction. No-one knew what it was. Taking my courage in both hands I ordered it, amid much hilarity from the rest of the party. When it came, all the sceptics were silenced; it looked as if I had ordered by far the tastiest item on the menu — it was beautiful! No-one else had followed my lead so there were a lot of envious faces.

So medicines apart, the next time you are out to dinner, and you don't know what to choose, why not try dowsing down the menu? You may well be pleasurably surprised, as I was.

So how does one dowse down a list for medicines? It is not as simple as using a medicine, witness and scale as I have previously described. What is needed is a convenient method that gives as little room for error as possible. This is why some dowsers use a hollow pendulum.

With a hollow pendulum, the witness (hair sample, etc.) from the patient is placed in the pendulum so that the pendulum is tuned to the patient. Never mind the theories, the main point is to use the concept as a working method. This could be described as constructing a thought-form such that the pendulum, with its witness, will only respond to the correct medicines for a particular patient. If you do not possess a hollow pendulum, then you could tie the sample on the pendulum or hold it in the same hand as the pendulum. This frees the other hand so that it can point to the list of medicines to be dowsed. I use a pencil as a pointer so that it is easy to see just which medicine is being pointed at. Figure 17 shows how this type of dowsing is done. The remedies are checked one-by-one until a positive reaction is obtained. There is no need to have read through all the actual remedies in the list first; one can dowse perfectly well using a list of remedies that you have never seen before.

If the index used is a homoeopathic *Materia Medica* (like

Figure 17. Dowsing down a list of remedies using a hair sample as witness

Allen's[16]), then short-cuts will be needed, again because of the sheer number of possible remedies. What I do is to check page-by-page with the question in my mind, 'Is there a suitable medicine listed on this page for this particular patient?' As soon as there is a positive reaction from one of the pages, then one can dowse carefully all the medicines on that page for which medicine or medicines are appropriate.

Always remember that you may obtain several answers. Note them all down if this happens. Assuming that just one positive answer had been noted, then the correct potency and dose rate will need to be determined. This can be done by using the scale, as mentioned on p. 92. In this case however a witness will be needed for the medicine as well as the patient, as it is unlikely that that particular remedy will be held in stock. A suitable witness need be nothing more than the name of the particular medicine written down on a piece of paper. The medicine witness is then put at the end of the scale at the point where the actual medicine would have been used. One can then dowse for the medicine dose rate and potency, as done previously when using the actual medicine. The answers should be checked in the reference book to verify that the results are reasonable. If the answers are never anything like the symptoms described in the book, then I would suggest that you are probably trying too hard. Alternatively, dowsing for homoeopathic medicines may just not be your forte.

What about the case where several answers are obtained? First of all, check to see if your dowsing reactions are all equally strong. If not, then it is nearly always the strongest one that is the best one to go for at the beginning. Assuming that they are all about equal strength, write down their names on separate pieces of paper and, using these as medicine witnesses, determine their strength against the patient witness using the ten-division scale (see Fig. 18) and

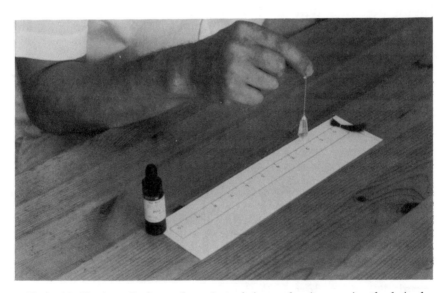

Figure 18. Testing a Bach remedy against a hair sample witness using the decimal scale

note down the readings you obtain. Then try using two remedy witnesses at the same time and see what the scale readings are. Do this for all possible combinations of two witnesses, then repeat using three medicine witnesses (assuming that three or more medicines gave a positive response). Then look for the single medicine or combination that gave the maximum response (reaction point nearest to the patient's witness). That medicine or combination of medicines will be the correct one to start with. The other medicines may well be appropriate later on in the treatment. Equally it may well be that either of two medicines would be equally effective on their own, so one of them would not be needed in the treatment.

Again a problem may arise. Suppose that the dowsing has thrown up six remedies, then the number of possible combinations of these six is large, and they will take a long time to dowse over. A short-cut method is needed for such times.

Put the medicine witness next to the patient witness and dowse over the pair with the mental question, 'Should this medicine be selected for the first treatment?' Check all medicines this way and you will have the correct medicine(s) to start treatment with.

I know that some homoeopathic purists may well say that only one remedy should be used at a time. Usually I find that my dowsing only turns up a single remedy, but quite often two appear. It is too easy to become carried away with theoretical ideas about what should or should not be done. In dowsing we are learning to use our intuition (inner intuition), not to follow the dogmas of others. I am not saying that one should deliberately flout rules or conventions, simply saying that when you know you can trust your dowsing, then trust it — even if it conflicts with some sacred cows. Ultimately what matters is the end result. Are you able to help yourself or those that come to you? If so, the manner of helping, the actual vehicle of healing, is immaterial. What matters is that it works.

CHAPTER 9

THE BACH FLOWER REMEDIES

The Bach Flower Remedies are used for treating emotional states, and their effect is to stimulate natural healing. Dowsing can be used to assist in selecting the appropriate remedies and for determining a correct emotional analysis.

About twenty years ago, when I first started learning about the healing applications of dowsing, the Bach Flower Remedies were not well known. I was introduced to them via a book by Beverley Nichols that had just been published[17], which mentioned how he had first come across them. He told how when he had visited Dr Aubrey Westlake, Dr Westlake's wife had dowsed over the Bach remedies for him. Apparently the meaning of the remedies was very close, perhaps almost too close for comfort.

The Bach remedies were stated to be for treating the individual's emotional states rather than dealing with physical symptoms. Indeed the whole story of Dr Bach makes interesting reading.

Dr Edward Bach was a skilled orthodox Harley Street physician, a pioneer in the field of immunology, yet he finally gave up this work to look for less aggressive methods of medical treatment. Bach felt strongly that orthodox medicine tried to bulldoze the body towards a state of health, and

---

17. Nichols, Beverley, *Powers That Be*, Jonathan Cape, 1966.

was therefore far too harsh in its effects. Bach knew intuitively that there must be a much gentler way of helping to heal the body, and that it might lie in the flowers of the countryside.

Bach left London and went to live in Norfolk, away from the hustle and bustle of city life. It was there that he found his inspiration for the remedies that are named after him. He saw the morning sun shining on the dew that had condensed overnight on a flower. He felt intuitively that such dew would have gained something of the healing properties of the flower, that he felt sure were there.

He therefore tried floating the fully opened flowers of the plant in a bowl of pure spring water, in full sunlight for a few hours. He then added an equal part of brandy to this water to act as a preservative, thus producing his 'mother tincture'. This he felt was far too concentrated for normal use, so it was then diluted by about 250 times to make the working stock essence.

It is one thing being able to produce medicines intuitively, but how do you know what they are for? Bach apparently did not know about the possibility of dowsing for answers, and again relied on his intuition. As will be seen in the next chapter, dowsing does not always give instant solutions to problems, so in reality, Bach probably followed the wisest path in the way that he determined the uses for his essences. This may sound condescending, but it is not meant to be so, in fact just the opposite. It is an easy option to feel that a system such as dowsing would have saved Bach much trouble; as I have learned to my cost this is not necessarily so.

Bach found his remedies in reverse, as it were. He did not go looking for remedies in flowers and then try to discover what the remedy was for. He took on himself, one at a time, a whole series of emotionally distressed states, or 'moods' as he called them, and then went looking for a flower that seemed to possess the property of alleviating that distress. Bach felt that if the stressful emotional mood could be taken from a patient, then the body's own defence system would be reactivated. His argument was that it was emotional stress that prevented natural healing taking place. For this reason he looked to reducing the level of stress in the patient rather than worrying about the symptoms that the patient happened to produce. Hence patients suffering from widely differing symptoms might well be treated with the same remedy.

Bach found an increasing number of flower remedies, but when he had twelve of them he felt that he had found all that were necessary. Later he realised that this was not so, and the list was finally expanded to thirty-eight separate remedies[18]. Bach's life story and discovery of the remedies makes fascinating reading and I would thoroughly recommend that anyone interested in this field should read his biography by Nora Weeks[19]

Apart from the thirty-eight separate remedies, there is one composite remedy which he called the Rescue Remedy. This comprises five of the remedies, and is specifically compounded for the reduction of shock. Whenever anyone is under sudden stress from accident, bereavement, etc., this remedy is remarkably effective. I can vouch for its effectiveness from experience. One particular time still remains fresh in my mind.

My two children were playing together in the garden when they were quite small. They had a paddling pool out, and were filling it with water. They must have decided that the water was rather too cool and the elder one went in to turn down the cold water. Unfortunately he turned it off just as the other one put the hosepipe down the front of his swimming trunks. The result was a loud scream and a

---

18.   Bach, Edward, *The Twelve Healers and Other Remedies*, C.W. Daniel, 1933, revised and reprinted many times.

19.   Weeks, Nora, *The Medical Discoveries of Edward Bach, Physician*, C.W. Daniel, 1963.

scalded small boy in a high degree of shock. We immediately put him in cool water and I rushed for the Rescue Remedy. We then took him to hospital, which took about fifteen minutes. When we started off he was still deadly white and in a state of shock, but by the time we got to hospital he was pink in colour and singing. There was little blistering and no after-effects such as nightmares or other signs of emotional damage. A remarkable case of healing.

From my own experience I can recommend the Bach Flower Remedies; they come high on my list of tools for helping people. There is one limitation with them, however, that of deciding which ones to use for any particular patient. Bach prescribed them by establishing the mood of the patient, and then from that result was able to prescribe the correct remedies. Herein lies the problem. It can be difficult to establish just what the emotional state of an individual really is. People become dab-hands at covering up their feelings, and it may take a lot of time to get the person to come-clean about how they really feel. I suspect that Dr Bach used his intuitive faculty to instinctively arrive at the correct remedies for any particular patient.

This is where dowsing can come in. Dowsing can be used to select the correct remedies for a patient, and then the specific remedies can be looked up to see what sort of emotional analysis is indicated. If in doubt, one can then talk to the patient to see if the results are correct. Like homoeopathic remedies, the incorrect one will normally do nothing, so if in doubt I rely on my dowsing as being accurate. What ultimately matters is whether or not the patient's condition improves.

I realise that in some areas, advocating dowsing with the Bach remedies is like waving a red rag to a bull. I have heard it said on several occasions, that one should follow rigorously the way that Dr Bach worked — anything else is dangerous heresy. What such advocates forget is that Dr Bach himself was a rebel. He rebelled against the methods of the time, feeling there were better ways. All I would

102

advocate is that with the upsurge of interest in medical uses of dowsing, this can be a perfectly valid way of discovering the correct remedies. Again, what matters is that the patient is helped: how it is actually done is of secondary importance to all concerned. Unfortunately, some people like to become experts in fields orthodox and unorthodox, and what is forgotten is that a dogmatic adherence to anything will ultimately destroy what was originally of value. One only has to look at how inspired religious teachers have had their words applied dogmatically, and the wars that have resulted from that dogmatism.

So how do we set about dowsing for the Bach remedies, and what sort of results may be expected? A full set of the Bach remedies costs somewhere in the order of £40, so they are not cheap. If you expect to work in the healing area, however, I would suggest that it could be money well spent. After all, just one private consultation with a medical consultant would set you back about the same amount. I would certainly recommend that everyone should have a bottle of Rescue Remedy to hand.

To all beginners I suggest dowsing with the actual remedies. It is perfectly possible to dowse from indexes, as was mentioned in the last chapter, but even so, most people find that they are less likely to make mistakes when using the actual essences.

The remedies can be dowsed over by using a graduated scale, as described in the previous chapter (see p. 92). In addition, one can dowse directly over each individual essence. This is the method that I normally use. There are only thirty eight of them in separate boxes, so I first of all dowse to see if I obtain a positive reaction from any of the individual boxes. If so, then I dowse over the individual remedies contained in a particular box. If I find that I am discovering responses from more than three remedies, then I check all those with a positive indication and use only those that give the three strongest responses.

I once stayed at a centre in Grasmere run by the late Aya

Harrison. I had given an impromptu lecture/demonstration on dowsing for the Bach remedies the previous evening, and we were discussing this the following tea-time. Two ladies had just arrived to stay for a few days and had missed my talk. They expressed great interest and someone asked if I would demonstrate to them how I worked. I retrieved my remedies and dowsed for one of the ladies to see what I found for her. The remedies that came up were for anguish and deep unhappiness. Everyone roared with laughter. There was this lady looking totally happy and contented, and my results were apparently all wrong.

'He is perfectly right,' she said, 'I have been very unhappy just recently, and I was in tears just before we left to come here. This is the face that I put on to the outside world, people aren't interested in the fact that I am so unhappy.' Everyone else there was shaken, particularly as a few worked professionally in the area of counselling. No-one had sensed the fact that the lady was so distressed.

This unfortunate situation was helpful to me, being a timely reminder that I could rely on my dowsing, even when all the evidence seemed to be against its indications.

I always dowse 'blind' over the Bach remedies. I look at the labels on the bottles after I have dowsed over them. That way, I cannot be influenced by knowing what a particular bottle contains. Too often in the past I have compromised my results by thinking, 'I am sure that this will be what is needed,' an auto-suggestion making sure that my dowsing gave just that result. With experience I am much less affected now by my thoughts, and quite often I experience results that are contrary to what I would expect. I take this to be a positive sign. I once dowsed for someone and obtained an answer that seemed to be far away from what I expected. I rechecked and obtained the same answer. I still couldn't believe it and rechecked again. The pendulum went off into what I can only call an angry positive swing. It was just as if it was saying to me, 'Why the hell don't you believe what I am telling you!' It was quite right, my conscious mind had got it all wrong.

As I mentioned, I always dowse blind over the Bach remedies, only looking afterwards at what the bottle contains. I still find it surprising that I find it necessary to use only a quite restricted range of the remedies. Some of them come up frequently, and some only occasionally. Remedies like Star of Bethlehem for shock are frequent results in my dowsing; others like Wild Oat for uncertainty, infrequent. I use about a third of the remedies on a regular basis. Incidentally, if dowsing was an illusion and a random process, this would not happen; on average all the remedies would be used equally.

So what are the practicalities of dowsing for the Bach remedies, and how much do you tell the patient? This latter point should be kept in mind because sometimes it may be counter-productive to tell someone all that you know.

First consider the dowsing. I find that if the person is there with me, then I have no problem in dowsing for the correct remedies. I just concentrate mentally on that person and what remedies will be appropriate for them. I leave the bottles in their boxes and touch them one at a time with a finger of my left hand, as I use my right hand for dowsing. Use whichever hand you find works best for your dowsing, and forget all talk about the left hand being unreliable or dangerous. As the left hand is connected to the right brain you might even expect it to work better, but I have no evidence for this at all.

I use the pendulum with a straight-line swing for neutral because this gives me the quickest response. I check each bottle carefully, watching for any change of direction of the pendulum. I take out all those remedies with a positive reaction as I dowse over the bottles. If the final tally is more than three, then I check for the size of the positive swing that I obtain from each of the remedies and pick out the strongest. Another way would be to dowse for the remedies that are needed in the first bottle of medicine. I would not recommend this for beginners, however, as it is best to keep any mental interference to an absolute minimum until more practice is gained.

Of course you could equally dowse for the remedies by using the calibrated scale method. I use the simple direct method because it works well for me. For some people, a method looking rather more 'scientific' can be helpful in quelling doubts from the rational mind. Also, a method using a rule will give relative strengths of response at the time of dowsing, removing the need for dowsing again if more than three remedies are obtained in the dowsing.

The next question is how should the remedies be prescribed now that they have been selected by dowsing? I assume that the medicine will need to be taken for about two weeks and therefore a preservative will be preferable. I accept that Dr Bach just used pure spring water, but having seen mould growths in old bottles of remedies I prefer to use alcohol as a preservative. I use a 50 per cent spring water 50 per cent vodka mixture as a base for the medicine. The Bach remedies use brandy as a base for the stock essences, but I feel that it is best to keep the basic preservative as simple and free from possible contamination effects as possible. Triple-distilled vodka is about as pure alcohol as one can easily obtain.

Almost fill a 10-ml dropper bottle (obtainable from any chemists) with the water–alcohol mixture. Then dowse for how many drops of each of the essences need to be added to this bottle. Again, one can either use a calibrated scale or just ask the question, 'How many drops of this essence are needed in this medicine bottle?' If you dowse this way, by asking a question, start off by mentally asking 'One drop?' then 'Two drops?' and so on. Note which gives the maximum swing to the pendulum and that is the number of drops that you will need. Usually this would be expected to lie between one and four drops. Anything more than five drops I would rate as suspect and would always dowse again from the beginning.

Repeat this process for any other essences that come up as

being required and add them to the dropper bottle. Screw on the top and then shake up the bottle well. Now dowse for the number of doses per day that will be necessary; this would be expected to lie between one and four. Finally check for the number of drops of medicine to be taken at each occasion. Again this would usually be between one and four.

The Bach remedies are taken in a little water, preferably before rather than after a meal. If one is in a hurry however the medicine can be dropped directly into the mouth. This latter technique can be invaluable with Rescue Remedy when it is needed as a matter of urgency.

Sometimes it is stated that the Bach remedies are completely safe and will have no adverse effects whatever. This I feel is a statement that is a shade too dogmatic. I would agree that one can take the Bach essences with no obvious adverse effects, however, as in homoeopathy, if one hits the correct remedy and dose spot-on, then there can be temporary aggravation of symptoms. I know this to be true because I have observed it on quite a few occasions. Again, as in homoeopathy, such symptoms are a positive sign, showing that the body is reacting favourably to the medicine and activating its healing processes.

Very occasionally (and I would stress the very), I have found a negative indication over one of the Bach remedies. On such occasions I do not use that particular essence, even though it might appear to fit the patient's condition. There are several possibilities, apart from incorrect dowsing: firstly, that particular medicine might make the patient feel sufficiently worse to actually hinder the healing process; secondly, it might be that its present use is inappropriate, even though it would be otherwise indicated. Perhaps other healing needs to take place before that particular remedy can have its desired effect. If in doubt, trust your dowsing. All the remedies and further information can be obtained from the Dr Bach Centre whose address is given in Appendix 1 (see p. 174).

The Bach remedies comprise a simple and comprehensive method of treating a whole variety of illnesses by tackling the emotional state of the patient. They are often effective, but equally, like all systems of medicine, sometimes they are of little or no value. If one believes that any system of medicine should be able to successfully treat all patients, then one is making a serious fundamental error. From my experience, some people will be assisted by one method or practitioner, others will benefit from other practitioners or forms of treatment. As my meditation teacher has said, 'If you are sufficiently skilled you can heal someone with a piece of wet lettuce!' This is not intended to put you off, merely to point out that you shouldn't be surprised if, in trying out the Bach (or any other) remedies, not all your clients improve. A success rate of 80 per cent major improvement is about what most practitioners achieve, some a bit more, some a bit less.

The main point is, if you try using a healing system of any sort, don't be surprised if you don't succeed all the time — no-one does.

I once talked to a healer in Hull about my healing experiences with laying-on-of-hands, wondering about apparent failures. 'When I first started healing, for the first two weeks I got really spectacular cures. I thought I was Jesus Christ!' he said. 'The next week everything went wrong and I discovered that I wasn't.'

Beginner's luck is common in all areas; don't let its disappearance get you down. Many people in the sphere of healing tend to dwell overmuch on those who do not respond, so remember, there is no immutable message from on high that says, 'Ye must cure all who come to you, of whatever diverse illnesses, or ye are a miserable failure, fit only to be cast into ye deepest bottomless pit.'

We are all human and our systems of treatment, however inspired, are not infallible. Remember this, keep a sense of humour and a sense of humility, and you will be able to help many others if you so wish. Dr Bach called his essences his helpers. That puts it in a nutshell. In working in healing we strive to help others, and anything that will help us is beneficial to our work. There are no guarantees of success, but if it is remembered that most alternative (complementary) practitioners work with patients where orthodox medical treatment has failed, then we will perhaps be a little more compassionate to ourselves.

CHAPTER 10
NEW FLOWER REMEDIES

The author has discovered and developed his own set of natural remedies, extending the approach taken by the Bach remedies. Dowsing can be used not only to determine appropriate cures but also to discover new medicines, their curative properties, and their applications. The Bailey Flower Essences are described in detail.

In the last chapter I described how Dr Bach used his intuitive faculty to determine which remedies were needed for the various emotional states that he experienced. When I read about this I wondered if he had found *all* the plants whose flowers had curative properties. After all, he had been quite specifically looking for plants that could help cure emotional problems. Perhaps there were others yet undiscovered.

This was about two years after I had developed an interest in dowsing, and with the typical enthusiasm of the recently converted, I started off dowsing round my garden for flowers with curative properties. I kept this thought firmly in my mind and finished up with a list of about ten.

I have always been interested in flowers, having had a love for them from an early age, so it seemed natural to me to see which of them had healing properties. My list of ten presented me with quite a few problems. Rather like the game 'Twenty Questions', if the question-and-answer type of dowsing is used, progress can only be made if some positive answers are obtained. Some of those flowers blocked every question I asked. All I could achieve was a succession of 'no' responses.

It went something like this:

Do you possess healing properties?	Yes
Can you be used with the Bach remedies?	Yes
Can I use you with any of my present patients?	No
Could I have used you with any of my past patients?	No
Might you be of any use with future patients?	A half no
Are you of any use for stress problems?	No

And so it went on, getting nowhere fast. Finally, after becoming completely desperate I did what I should have done much sooner: I looked at the first question that I had asked. 'Do you possess healing properties?' I realised that it was far too wide as the whole of the animal and plant kingdoms were included in my question.

So I rephrased it. 'Do you possess healing properties for humans?' Immediately the difficult flowers gave a 'no' response. That left me with the rest that gave firm positive answers.

My troubles were not over as I could not dowse sensible answers to what the remedies were for. I exhausted my list of illnesses, symptoms, emotions, everything I could think of, and all I could discover was a succession of firm no or weak yes answers. Yes, I could make up remedies using Bach's sun method, floating the flowers in full sunlight in a glass bowl of spring water. Yes, I could use alcohol as a preservative (I found a rather better response on vodka than brandy). Yes, I could use them with the Bach remedies. Yes, I would find them useful. No, I could not find out what they were for!

I had come up against the fundamental problem of question-and-answer type of dowsing, for it is one thing to hold a pendulum over something and ask a question, it is quite another when you can't find the right sort of question to ask. Try as I would, I couldn't find the way in. My rational mind came up with endless questions, but they all met a brick wall, no response.

I became terribly frustrated, yet the more frustrated I was, the less I seemed to be able to find any helpful response. Finally I gave up trying and I gave in to the remedies. I made them up as Bach had done with his remedies, marked their names on them, and put them with my Bach remedies. I then waited to see what happened. I had discovered six of them altogether by the summer: rhododendron, Welsh poppy, soapwort, buttercup, bluebell and foxglove.

When a new patient came I checked all the Bach remedies and then my own, and much to my surprise my own remedies were indicated as suitable about one time in three. I checked my dowsing carefully and obtained firm positive answers about using the remedies with the Bach ones. Taking my courage in both hands I made up the composite remedies and waited to see what happened.

I appreciated that the essences were, like Bach's, of homoeopathic potency, so there was no real risk of causing any damage. Nevertheless I cautioned my patients to watch out for aggravation of symptoms, and to ring me up if they had any problems. I need not have worried, all was well. Indeed the results I was achieving when using the new remedies were promising, and one case in particular stood out. For this particular patient the only remedy indicated was rhododendron — one of mine. The patient had suffered a nervous breakdown just after taking his final degree and he had never recovered. He lived at home with his mother and no treatment had had any beneficial effect. He had tried to work but just could not concentrate and so had been unemployed for several years. He was depressed, and had been diagnosed as suffering from a form of mental illness.

His recovery was amazing. Within a week he was feeling much better and within six months he was holding down a full-time job and was really happy. I rechecked my dowsing for rhododendron. 'Is it of use in some cases of mental illness?' I obtained a half-hearted yes and so was still no nearer.

I was therefore in the position of having some new flower essences that were obviously useful, but I could not find out what they were for. They were indicated frequently when dowsing for the remedies that were needed for a patient, but there was no obvious pattern linking them to either illness or emotional states.

However the fact remained that they were useful and helpful, so I just carried on using them, hoping that in due course I would discover what they were for. At times I had the urge to dowse for further remedies, and slowly the numbers of them built up.

Often I would find a new remedy when I had a particularly difficult case to deal with. For instance, on one occasion I could not find a suitable remedy for a friend of mine, nothing seemed to fit, my dowsing giving a series of 'nos' to anything I checked. It was during the spring, and I went away to run a weekend course in the country near Evesham. That Saturday afternoon, during a break in the course, I saw a bank of wood anemones by the river. Something inside me 'knew' that they would make the remedy that I was looking for. Dowsing confirmed that inner knowing so I set about making up some of the remedy from the flowers. I found a glass bowl, put the flowers in it with some bottled spring water and left it out in the sun. Two hours later I collected it and added an equal quantity of vodka as a preservative.

That remedy was immediately helpful when given to my friend. It was only later on when I discovered that this particular remedy is effective in dealing with problems of long standing — genetic or from previous lifetimes depending on your point of view.

I was now faced with a steadily increasing armoury of remedies, compatible with the Bach ones, effective, but not many ideas as to what they were really for. All I knew was, that when selected by dowsing, they were useful in helping

113

people to regain their health. At one level, that is all that matters. Nevertheless I found it frustrating, particularly when people asked me what the remedies were for.

INTUITIVE KNOWLEDGE

Over an eleven-year period I had come up with about twenty-six new flower essences. I used them on a regular basis, but was still no nearer finding out just what they were for. Then circumstances arose that completely changed my life. I went to York to hear a meditation teacher give a talk. It was called 'Meditation in Everyday Life'.

Now I had previously, reluctantly, done some meditation. While meditating I had experienced vivid images that seemed to have significance for me. Yet in a way it all seemed to be rather divorced from my normal life, rather too esoteric. At the lecture, here was someone talking in a completely different vein. The talk was saying that unless one's meditation practice affected all one's life, how one walked, talked, sat, even flushed the loo, then it was not working. Meditation should integrate one's life so that everything one did became more skilful.

I was entranced. Here was someone talking commonsense. It struck a deep resonant chord in me. I had always felt that orthodox religion and the meditation methods that I had tried were somehow separate from life. Here was someone saying that meditation should affect the very core of everyday life, making it easier and more joyful.

The upshot was that I started to work with this teacher, who was called John Garrie. This is not the place to go further into his method of working except to state that it is now the basis of my everyday life, and he was quite right, it really does work.

One of John's long-term students was a lady called Caroline. She was direct and also attractive. I had told her about

114

my remedies, and went to see her in London to discuss them with her. Maybe I had ulterior motives, in fact I am sure I had, but whatever my motivation, circumstances in this case led me to see Caroline.

She was interested in the remedies, and particularly in my lack of knowing what they were for. I remember she fixed me with a searching look and said, 'Arthur, you have created these essences, so deep down you must know what they are for. I have worked as a secretary so I can take things down at speed. I will take out the essences one at a time and read out the names. You lie back and relax, and tell me just whatever comes into your mind. I will write it all down and then we can see what you intuit about them.'

I thought I had been well and truly rumbled. I had that uncomfortable feeling that she knew I could give the answers, and worse she would not let up until I agreed. So that was the way that it was. I lay back with my eyes closed and listened to her reading out the names.

Much to my surprise, words came into my head. Phrases like 'cooling warmth', 'comfortably bewitched', 'breaking through into new levels of consciousness', and so on. When I saw the final list I was amazed. It all made good sense and corresponded well with the patients I had seen. This was the first breakthrough in understanding the remedies.

I now had a further problem. It is one thing reading about clairvoyance and perhaps half believing it, it is something quite different to find yourself actually doing it. Once again I had experienced something that my rational mind found quite unacceptable and I went home in a state of shock. I now had a list of what the remedies were for, but I was not at all happy about how I had obtained it, for I hadn't really believed that such things could work in this way.

On the positive side I could now talk more freely to other people about the remedies. I did however tend to keep quiet about how I had discovered the information, and was rather embarrassed by it all. If questioned too deeply, I muttered things about dowsing for the answers. Not true, but at that time I could not cope with the information that I was being presented with.

There was no doubt that the remedies could greatly help to alleviate symptoms, to make people feel better; that I knew from experience. What I now knew was that they operated in a different way than just by removing symptoms, they helped people at some deeper level.

It was about five years later, owing to the work that I was doing with my meditation teacher, that the whole healing pattern suddenly appeared to become clear to me. The essences were for *attitudes of mind*, how we view the external and the inner worlds, not for the emotional states themselves, which the Bach remedies dealt with, but for that which comes before. I realised that the remedies were to help the patient to let go of old outmoded belief patterns, desires, rigid ways of thinking. In fact everything that gets in the way of personal freedom and living a free and happy life.

At long last I had found the answers that I had been looking for. I realised that I could not have arrived at those conclusions before, because such concepts had not even entered my head. It had been a case of 'knowing in part and seeing in part'.

At the present count there are thirty six of these essences that I use (see Fig. 19) and have made available to those who wish to use them (see Appendix 1, p. 174). I always dowse for them, although it is possible to prescribe them purely from counselling the patient. I find that it is easier to dowse first and then talk to the patient about what the remedies suggest. If someone is sitting on their creative potential, then helping them to see the possibility of changing their lives for themselves could be of great help to them. The essences will be of help, yes, but helping the patient to motivate themselves will greatly help the healing process.

Deep within us there is a bright point of illumination: this is the area of the psyche where everything we need to know is available to us. Unfortunately we tend to be so busy with

116

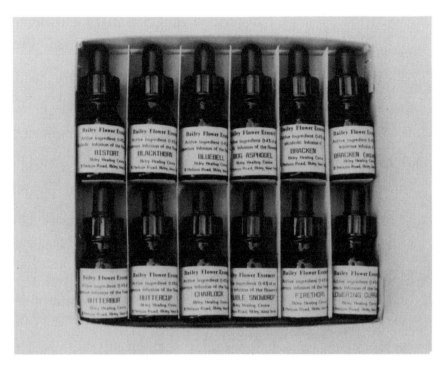

Figure 19. The Bailey Flower Essences

life and our opinions that we never give ourselves sufficient time and space to become aware of what it can tell us. Between this inner knowing and all our outer life — our attitudes, desires, hopes, conditionings and belief structures — there inevitably forms a credibility gap. It is this gap that creates emotional stress, believing one thing yet knowing deep down that we are deluding ourselves.

Emotional stress causes a whole set of symptoms. There are changes in body chemistry which can seriously affect the auto-immune system and virtually all bodily functions besides. Also the mental stress creates chronic muscle tensions that will affect breathing, posture, facial expression and the whole attitude to the physical body.

Finally come all the physical symptoms that one might complain of. Agreed, some of these can be caused by factors like incorrect diet as I described in Chapter 6. However there is no doubt that the majority of illnesses stem from the mind and its attitude to the world.

All three are interlinked, so healing at any level will tend to help the others. The real root, however, is our way of looking at things. This is not necessarily the best place to start treatment, but there is no doubt that until a person can live at peace with themselves and the world, then the body will reflect the conflicts that result.

These particular essences have been my teachers. I have learned much from my struggles to understand them. I know others who use them and gain help from them. Ultimately all that can be asked for any system is 'Does it work?' I find that these essences work for me. The fact that one cannot say *why* flower essences work is a purely intellectual problem. It may be forgotten that the patient is mainly concerned with being helped, the actual method of helping is of secondary importance.

Like homoeopathy, the operation of the healing process is open to debate. We must never allow such debates to get in the way of the real object — helping people to become healed and whole.

CHAPTER 11

DISTANT HEALING

The origins of Radionics are considered, and the use of dowsing in combination with this method of distant healing described. The author comes to some controversial conclusions — it works but not in the way you may think it does, as the laws of physics are defied time and time again.

One of the methods of healing at a distance is the technique called 'Radionics'. Before we look at this method of working, it will be as well to consider the origin of such an unlikely method of working.

It all started with a Dr Abrams before the last war. He was working with patients and discovered that the sound that he heard on his stethoscope, when percussing the abdomen of his patients, seemed to vary depending on the illness of the patient. Apparently he was using a primitive form of dowsing, using the patient's abdomen as a sounding board! This in itself was quite a remarkable observation, but he proceeded to take the matter further. He realised that the patient was in this context only an instrument, so he replaced the patient with a diaphragm, which worked just as well. This later developed into a small diaphragm made of thin rubber which was used as a 'stick' pad rather than something to be struck. The idea was that on stroking the pad, if the answer was 'yes' then the finger would stick to it, a 'no' would result in the finger sliding over the pad surface.

The use of the pad was just another method of dowsing, a small increase in finger tension being all that was necessary to make the finger stick to the rubber instead of sliding over it. Nowadays people use pendulums, but the stick pad was used for a long time before this, it being thought that it responded to a different phenomenon to dowsing, to give a meaningful response.

A breakthrough came when Abrams wondered whether his results were due to some sort of natural vibration that could be tuned in to with electrical apparatus. He therefore built a machine which consisted of a set of rheostats (electrical variable resistors) of the type that were then used to control the filament current of radio valves. The rheostats were provided with knobs that were calibrated. The set of rheostats was wired in series, and the end connection terminated underneath the 'stick' pad. The patient touched a connection to the other end of the rheostats and the dials were adjusted one at a time from their zero positions until a 'stick' reaction was observed. With six knobs this gave a six-digit code. What Abrams found was that the settings of the knobs were always the same for patients suffering from the same illness. Thus if Bovine TB gave dial settings of 415628, then this code could be written down in a book. If a patient was checked with the instrument and settings of 415628 were obtained, then the diagnosis could be obtained from looking up the 'rate' in the codes that had been compiled. In that case Bovine TB would therefore be the diagnosis.

The rates were compiled quite simply by determining the instrument settings from a patient with a known illness. These were cross-checked with results from other patients and the instrument settings were then recorded in a book. This formed the standard set of rates for the instrument.

Because the instrument was manufactured with a black ebonite front panel (typical of scientific instrument practice before the last war), it became known as the 'Black Box'. This was many years before aeroplane flight recorders appeared that were given the same name. At this stage, the Black Box was basically a diagnostic instrument which could be used when symptoms were confusing. Providing that the rates had been compiled carefully, then the results obtained were usually accurate. It was assumed that the instrument was somehow in tune with the illness, the circuits resonating with the patient.

The next stage was to remove the need for the patient to touch the instrument. A sample holder was provided that was connected to the end of the box circuit remote from the stick pad. It was found that the instrument worked just as well when a sample from the patient (sputum, urine or blood) was placed in this container. Distant diagnosis was now possible; the instrument had no longer to be brought to the patient.

The final breakthrough came when the reverse process was tried. As the system could be resonated to the patient to provide diagnosis, could it be worked in reverse? In other words could the oscillatory circuits, set up by the rheostats, be tuned to another rate which would beneficially affect the patient?

This was done by taking a patient with a known illness. The instrument was then retuned one rheostat at a time, checking for a 'stick' that would correspond with a treatment rate. Hopefully this second rate would broadcast radiations back to the patient that would help in the healing process. This was tried, and much to their surprise it seemed to work. The patients given treatment from the Black Box did get better more rapidly than those without such treatment.

Another set of rates was therefore produced to go in the record book. These rates were those required to broadcast the healing treatment back to the patient. It was from this background that the Radionic instrument was born and it can now be seen where the term Radionic came from. It was derived from the assumption that the box worked with radiations, both from and to the patient.

Various people developed this idea further from its initial beginnings. George De La Warr was perhaps the best known name in this field after the war. The De La Warr Black Box

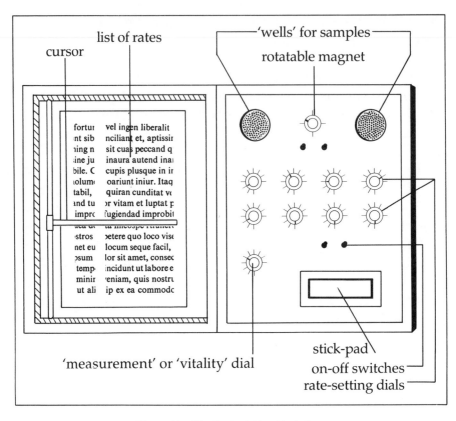

Figure 20. The De La Warr Black Box

(see Fig. 20) was one of the best known boxes in the UK at that time. De La Warr developed the box further and even produced a Radionic camera which produced photographic prints from samples obtained from patients.

Not everyone managed to use the box. There was a well publicised court case where a lady took the De La Warrs to court because she said that she had suffered severe mental illness from trying to make the box work, and she claimed it was a fraud. She was supported on legal aid to pursue the prosecution, but the De La Warrs won their case. The judge said that although he had been completely unable to grasp how the box worked, the evidence that had been produced to support its effectiveness was overwhelming. Although

122

the De La Warrs had won, British justice being what it is, they were almost made bankrupt from fighting the case in court.

The Black Box, in all its different variations, works. Of that there is no real doubt, but how does it work? When the stick pad was replaced with a plate, over which one could dowse with a pendulum, the resonance ideas began to look a bit thin. Also the use of rheostats was peculiar from an engineering standpoint because resistance damps out electrical oscillations, not tunes them in. In short, there is no orthodox explanation for the design whatever. So like dowsing, we have a problem. It should not work, yet unrepentantly it does so!

I wondered about this when I first read about Radionics, and I built myself a Black Box using resistors and calibrated scales which worked for me when using a pendulum. Very peculiar. I tried changing the wiring inside and said to myself, 'The box will continue to work.' The box still worked for me. Finally I made the ultimate leap, I made my Grey Box.

The Grey Box (see Fig. 21) is so called because it was built in a box that was already painted grey. It has a grey top panel and knobs with calibrated escutcheons. It has a sample holder and a telescopic aerial for broadcasting treatments. I also provided it with selector switches so that its mode of operation can be changed. For instance it can be switched from analyse to treatment modes without resetting the rates: they are the same for both, which saves looking things up. This has the additional advantage that one does not even need a book of rates, unless you wish to know what the patient's problems are. All one need do is to dowse for the settings of each of the nine dials in turn, with the patient's witness (hair sample, etc.) in the sample holder. When all the dials are set, then one extends the aerial rod and changes the switch from 'analyse' to 'treat'. It works very well, but there is just one problem. There is nothing inside it! No potentiometers, no wiring, nothing! This can

Figure 21. The 'Grey' Box

be seen in Figure 22 where a side view of the top of the box can be seen.

I was not the first one to do this. I discovered a few years after I made the box that an American lady had been prosecuted in court for selling 'black' boxes with nothing in them but sawdust. The fact that they apparently worked was immaterial. It was just as well for the De La Warrs that their box looked more scientific, and therefore more believable.

We have this unfortunate idea that unless something has a rational explanation or *looks rational in its appearance,* then it cannot work. I am sure that many people have come into healing through Radionics because the boxes have an impressive setting-up procedure and look technical. My experience is that they are an impressive crutch which may well be of use if we doubt our own legs will support us. However *there is no magic in the box.* The real magic is inside

124

the thing that is called 'myself'. All of us possess powers and abilities that far exceed our dreams. What we need is the confidence and wisdom to use them.

I know many people who have started off with Black Boxes and have ended up by discarding them. Not because they could not get results with them, no, it was because they found that they could get equally good results without them.

Now this may all sound a bit negative and anti-radionics. It is not meant to be so. It is meant to show how easy it is to be carried away by pseudo-technology and miss the basic points in the process.

If you rent or buy a Radionic or other type of Black Box, you will find that it comes complete with a book of rates for that particular machine. This is to save you the laborious

Figure 22. End view of the top panel of the Grey Box showing absence of any functional wiring

process of working them out for yourself. However, like other dowsing systems, herein lies a problem. As was mentioned in Chapter 2, factors like specific lengths of pendulums, lengths and directions of 'fundamental rays', rates, etc., tend to be personal — independent testing of dowsers gives different figures for each person. So how does a published book of rates work?

It seems to be that if one accepts that the rates in that particular book are correct, then those rates will work for you. Curiouser and curiouser, as Alice said.

It is these apparent conflicts that are widely exploited by people who are desperately trying to expose dowsing, etc., as a fraud. I must admit that it all does seem to be strange and can appear to be the unacceptable face of dowsing.

As with so many situations, one must be careful before jumping to premature conclusions. It is temptingly easy to pooh-pooh ideas because one does not like to accept their implications. So, keeping this in mind, let us have a look at the question of rates as a typical example.

There have been many different Radionic machines manufactured over the years. The late Malcolm Rae was forever producing larger and larger machines; one of these had no fewer than forty-nine dials to set up. The idea seemed to be that the more complex the machine, the more selective it could be and therefore the more effective. Amongst these machines there were quite a few that had the same number of settable dials with the same number calibrations (usually 0 to 9). One investigator did the correct thing to investigate the much vexed question of rates — he obtained two machines with the same number of dials complete with their respective books of rates. He then asked experienced Radionic-machine operators to use the new machines and do analyses of samples from patients. He found that the results were good, correlating closely with what was known of the patients. However what he had not told the operators was that some of them were using the manufacturer's set of rates for the machine, some of them

126

were using the rates (which were different) for the other machine. The accuracy was just as high when using the incorrect book of rates.

The conclusion therefore appears to be that we can either produce our own set of rates, or use those prepared by someone else. Providing that we accept those rates as being correct, then they will work for us.

At this point I appreciate that all attempts at a rational explanation seem to fade into non-existence. How on earth can one know what lies inside a book when one has never opened it? Yet the fact remains that it works. In reality it is really no more impossible than dowsing down an index of remedies. It is uncomfortable that it works, but I have proved its efficacy on innumerable occasions when dowsing for a particular patient's needs. I repeat, what matters is that it works. The human being has far more powers than can be explained logically to the satisfaction of the rational mind. The intuitive, illogical, feeling-based, feminine aspects of our natures is a reality, whether we be man or woman. Successfully using an incorrect book of rates is just such a case. The pseudo-scientific person will refuse to accept this, and from this has arisen the concept that there are several rates that will work for any particular purpose. Therefore in Radionic circles there arise arguments about which is the best rate to use for a particular purpose. I suggest that this is merely a sop to the rational mind — trying to make respectable something which is linked to a different type of reality.

Within the Radionic field ideas exist that Radionics is absolutely safe, that it cannot possibly cause harm. Now such concepts are always suspect. If one has the power to affect things, then unwise action can always cause harm, even if one's motives may seem to be for the good. In any case, what is harm and what is good? All too often such things are viewed only from an emotional standpoint with a failure to see the wider implications.

One peach farmer in the USA was suddenly confronted with a plague of caterpillars which would have destroyed his entire crop later in the year. Rather than use poison sprays he used his Radionic box. He dowsed for a rate that would clear his trees of the caterpillars, set up the rate on the box, and waited. Within a week all the caterpillars had died off. When reported, this upset many people who had had the cosy thought that Radionics was a benign method of healing; some said that it was an outrageous use of the box. Yet this is too simplistic a view. We need to look wider.

Suppose it was *your* livelihood at stake and was threatened by the caterpillars, what then? From a safe position it is only too easy to criticise or to say how things should be done; when one is directly in the firing line, things look different. I remember my father saying that if the generals in the First World War had ever spent time in the trenches in the front line, where he had been, then there was no way they would have made such stupid decisions as they did.

There are two approaches to trying out a black-box method of healing. First of all you could go on a short introductory course to develop a feel for it. If it still seems to be what you want to do, then rent a box and see how you fare. The Radionic Association (address in Appendix 1, see p. 174) would be the best point to start your investigations, as they cater for all Radionic training requirements in a thorough manner. Your dowsing does need to be reliable; unless you can obtain consistent 'yes' and 'no' answers, then your Radionic results are likely to be equally variable.

Secondly, you could try a do-it-yourself approach. You could make up a box like the one that I made, but this needs a source of suitable materials and a basic set of engineering tools. The cheapest method of all is that evolved by a dowser from Northern Ireland who saw my Grey Box. In his method you throw the box away!

Take a long strip of paper, say 20 cm long by 4 cm wide, and write down the numbers from 0 to 9 along it. This is what you will dowse over. On a separate sheet of paper write down the name of the patient. Decide what length of code you are going to use; I am sure that four digits is sufficient, but you may like to use six or eight to fit in with some of the commercial systems. Take a suitable sample from the patient (hair, etc.) in the left hand, assuming that you dowse with the right, and dowse along the set of numbers until you find a reaction. You need to have in mind the question, 'I am dowsing for a treatment rate for this particular patient.' Write down the number, then dowse down the numbers for the next number, write it down, and so on. You will finally finish up with a four-, six- or nine-figure number which represents the rate needed to treat the patient. Put the patient's sample on top of the number that you have written down, and that is all there is to it. Nothing more to do.

Recheck the patient the following day, and if the numbers keep the same or alter, either way is fine. When you dowse all zeros, this indicates that there is nothing more you can do to help in that particular way.

If you are not happy with imposing a fixed number of blanks to fill in, then make a numbered strip as above but with an extra place marked 'end', as is shown in Figure 23. Dowse as before, but dowse starting with the end label. Keep writing down the numbers until you obtain a reaction from the end place. The numbers you have written down are the required treatment rate. In this case, a reaction from the end place at the start of dowsing will indicate that no further treatment of this type will be of assistance to the patient.

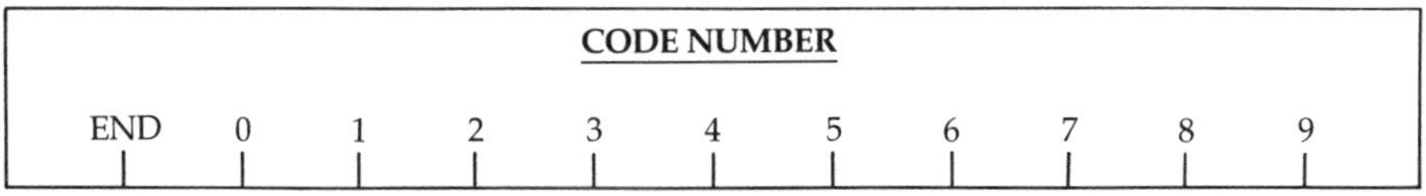

CODE NUMBER										
END	0	1	2	3	4	5	6	7	8	9

Figure 23. Decimal scale for distant treatment with number codes

DEFYING THE LAWS OF PHYSICS

So far in this chapter we have looked at the black-box approach to healing at a distance, a technique which owes nothing to radiations in the conventional sense. In physics there is a law called the Inverse Square Law. This says that radiations of energy, of whatever form, radiated from a single point source, will reduce in intensity depending on the square of the distance away from that source. In other words if the receptor is twice as far away from that source, then it will only receive one quarter of the initial energy level; ten times as far, one hundredth. If the Black Box used any form of measurable radiation, then the dose that the patient received would reduce rapidly with distance. Yet I and many others know from personal experience that this is not the case. One can satisfactorily treat people on the opposite side of the world.

It is factors such as these that critics use against Radionics and the Black Box approach to healing. It is just the same problem as we saw earlier with dowsing and the use of the term radiesthesia. All one can say is that if there is radiation, then it is certainly not of a type known to orthodox science.

So what do we really know? First, that it works. I and many others know that it works repeatedly, from personal experience. Secondly, like dowsing, the accuracy seems to be much greater when there is a real need, rather than experimenting with it out of idle curiosity. Thirdly, there is some sort of information, and therefore energy interchange between the practitioner and the patient. In this latter case I am assuming that we take it to be the practitioner rather than the box that is communicating with the patient. Fourthly, the link between the patient and practitioner must be intelligent. Somehow the information reaches only the person selected for treatment — like a personal telephone wire rather than a broadcast treatment that everyone else would react to. There is nothing in the box that can achieve this last property, therefore the magic, in the broadest sense of this word, must lie in the practitioner.

To our orthodox logical left brain we now really do have a 'tiger by the tail'. Personal 'telephone links' to other people, selectable at will — whatever next! Rubbish! The rational mind will often put all manner of blocks up rather than accept that we have another, and in many ways superior aspect of intelligence *that is not within its comprehension*. This is particularly the case with men. In giving talks about these subjects I usually find that it is the men who give all the vociferous opposition and the women who look at me in puzzlement, wondering why I feel that I have to try to justify what is, after all, so obvious. Uncomfortable though it may be, the Black Box approach works, as I and many others can testify.

I well remember my first experience on having an analysis conducted on a Tansley Box. The late Dr David Tansley worked extensively in the field of Black Boxes and produced his own, beautifully made box. This could measure the activity of the chakras (energy centres of the body which correspond to different levels of consciousness) and related to them, rather than working on the more physical basis of the De La Warr Box. These chakras are energy centres known originally to eastern healers and mystics and can give a good guide to the state of a person's health. They can also be used for healing and other purposes[20].

It was at the time when I was learning about this area that I met Bruce McManaway. My health was not too good, so after giving me some contact healing he suggested that Betty McPherson, a neighbour of his, should provide an analysis for me on her Tansley Box. All she needed was a hair sample, so I sent one off to her. Bruce contacted me about a week later to say that he had the results of her analysis and could he meet me on the way down to London

---

20. Iyengar, B.K.S., *Light on Yoga*, Unwin Paperbacks, 1976.

to discuss it. I was puzzled about the secrecy, but met him at a hotel on the A1 near Wetherby. He did not give me the analysis but read it out to me. Much was quite straightforward and extremely accurate. It was just as if someone who had known me for a long time was giving me an accurate character reading. What I had not appreciated was that the Transley Box analysis gave results not of physical illnesses but of emotional states and attitudes of mind, rather like the Bach remedies. Betty McPherson's results were very, if uncomfortably, accurate. I then found out why Bruce did not want to give them to me written down.

'It says here,' he said, wriggling rather uncomfortably in his seat, 'that you may well be a homosexual.' He was obviously embarrassed by having to say this to me. Remember that it was in the mid-sixties and that both he and I had grown up in a society where homosexuality was never even mentioned, it was far too embarrassing — heterosexual sex was bad enough. Thank goodness we have left those claustrophobic days behind, even if things did then swing rather too far in the opposite direction.

I was amused rather than embarrassed. At one level the analysis was right, I have always had a strong female aspect to my being. It manifested in various ways, being used as a shoulder to cry on, love of colour, interest in people and what made them tick, many things. Such sensitivity in a man, if not supported by a strong masculine side, can often lead to problems, particularly when relating to women. Women looking for a strong male can appear cruel to such a person, ridiculing their lack of masculine positivity. It is small wonder that such men often take to the sexual company of other men for safety and protection, rather than trying to develop their own masculinity.

For me it was lucky that I had not gone down the homosexual path, for in retrospect it would have worked against me being able to develop my own male aspects. Nevertheless Betty's analysis was basically correct; I was living with too little personal male energy in my life.

Incidentally, the British Radionic Society at that time had outlawed David Tansley and his box, and it was the De La Warr Box that was the approved model. David was a *persona non grata*. As with many fringe areas, the Radionic Society had developed its own orthodoxies and beliefs of what and what was not acceptable. Perhaps because David Tansley was marketing boxes in competition with theirs, David was definitely 'out'.

Later on the Society apparently realised that as he was becoming more and more successful, and better and better known, they were on a hiding to nothing. The conclusion was that they did an about face and welcomed him into the fold. Later, he became their president.

Earlier I showed how we could throw the box away and just dowse for a number code. How about the final possibility — throw away the code? After all it looks as if the intelligence behind distant 'box' healing is dependent on the operator rather than the box. Perhaps a code is not needed at all.

Try out the following and see what happens. Take a hair or other sample from someone who requires healing. Even a signature will do if nothing else is available. Hold a pendulum over the sample and relax. Inform your mind that you wish the pendulum to rotate for as long as healing energies are being accepted by the person requiring healing. Keep the thought in mind that you are transmitting healing energy to the other person for them to make use of *if they so wish*. Then watch your pendulum. All being well it should start rotating. Just keep relaxed and watch, *and don't try to do anything*. If you wish to visualise energies leaving you, or feel a link with the other person, fine, but the main thing is just to allow good will towards the other person to exist. Nothing more.

All being well, after a short time the pendulum will slow down and stop rotating. If it is still 'running' after five minutes, the odds are that you are trying rather than just letting it happen. That is it! Nothing more to do, no complex rituals, no striving to help the other person, no ego trip either. Just you offering healing to the other person and checking with the pendulum to see when you can move on to the next thing that you need to do.

You will know instinctively when to move on to the next patient needing treatment. It seems too simple. Yet it works. Dare I say it, but when you become competent, then you can even throw the pendulum away.

So use a box by all means, as you may find it helpful. Remember that it takes time to develop expertise and confidence, and always bear in mind however that *you* are the essential ingredient, and that it is your good will towards the person needing healing that is paramount. Good will is essential; trying only gets in the way. It is also important to be relaxed and not to be anxious, so practising meditation or relaxation can help enormously. The best healers that I know seem almost offhand about it all. Not that they don't care — no. It is simply that they do not identify themselves as being healers; they only see themselves as someone who is able to help others from time to time. The true magic comes from relaxation and a non-identification with whatever healing takes place.

CHAPTER 12

LEFT BRAIN – RIGHT BRAIN

How does dowsing work? The answer may lie in the functioning of the brain, and the different types of responses given by each hemisphere. Dowsing results from a reaction on the dowser, not on the dowsing instrument, which is used to amplify the dowser's own intuitive unconscious knowledge.

By now it should be apparent that the activity of dowsing cannot be explained on a rationally acceptable basis. There is no 'reason' for its existence. Like my clairvoyant experiences in discovering the meanings of the flower essences, such things feel uncomfortable in a society that seems to be dominated by logic. It is easy to become disheartened and wonder if one is just imagining things after all. Did all those people really get better because of your help, or was it all just coincidence, the odd millions-to-one coincidence?

The problem lies in our too-ready acceptance of the logical side of our nature, and believing that that is all there is to it. The idea of an intuitive side is still viewed with derision in some quarters. Yet scientific research has shown that we are indeed more than just a logical 'meat-machine'.

It is therefore appropriate at this point to look deeper into the differences between left and right sides of the brain, to see if an intuitive side does indeed exist.

A significant breakthrough in understanding something of the brain's functions came when research was done into some cases of severe epilepsy. It was noticed that in some patients the 'electrical storm' of epilepsy started in one hemisphere of the brain, transferred to the other and then seemed to oscillate between the two. There is a bundle of nerve fibres called the *corpus callosum* that links the two hemispheres of the brain, the function of which was not understood. It appeared that this was the link that was propagating the epilepsy. The patients were seriously ill, so it was decided to operate on some of them, severing the *corpus callosum* to see what would happen.[21]

Most of the patients were much better and seemed normal — so what was the function of the linking nerves? It soon came to light. The *corpus callosum* enables the two halves of the brain to 'talk' to each other.

The people who had had the operation showed clearly, for the first time, just what the functional differences were between the two hemispheres of the brain. It was already known that the nerves from the right hemisphere connected to the left side of the head and body, the left hemisphere being connected to the right side. The large difference in processing between the left and right hemispheres was not known.

Considering one of the patients who had had the split-brain operation, if someone whispered into their right ear (connected to the left brain) then they could understand the words, but not know who was speaking. Whispering into the left ear they knew who was speaking but could not understand the words!

Similar occurrences happened with the eyes. An experiment was set up with the patient viewing two screens, one for the left eye only, one for the right eye only, so arranged that the images coincided. Someone with normal vision would just see one picture if the same image was on both screens. The patients were then shown a set of slides,

---

21.   Lishmann, W.A., 'Split Minds: A Review of the Results of Brain Bisection in Man', *British Journal of Hospital Medicine*, 2, 477–84, 1969.

sometimes the same to both eyes, sometimes different. When the images were different, it was always the right eye that dominated and the patient reported the image presented to that eye — it was if the left was blind, yet it was seeing and interpreting visual information.

This was really emphasised when the right eye was presented with something innocuous like a picture of cows grazing in a field, while the left eye, however, was presented with a photograph of a nude. In the words of one experimenter, 'A kind of sneaky grin would spread over the face of the patient, and they would look rather embarrassed.' When asked what they could see, they answered, 'Cows grazing in a field.' 'What are you embarrassed about then?' 'I just don't know!' was the reply.

The patients were reacting emotionally to visual stimuli that they could not see. Now this is pretty weird however you consider it. It shows that the right brain can interpret images emotionally without the observer actually having the experience of seeing what is there to be seen.

Further work confirmed all these factors and more. The left brain, for the great majority of people, is concerned with what is termed 'linear processing': subjects such as logic, mathematics, language. It is also concerned with time, interpreting this as a linear phenomenon that flows steadily by. Also the left brain is concerned with such personal characteristics as aggressiveness and being sure of what one is doing because it appears to be 'logically' correct, in fact all the characteristics that have been typically associated with the masculine.

The right brain is concerned with different functions. It is concerned with experiencing events as a complete whole rather than a set of logically related but separate pieces. It does not appear to be restricted by time or distance; it feels and is the seat of the emotions; it is the side connected with creativity, producing results that are not necessarily a logical development from what has gone before; appreciation of art and music predominantly lie in this hemisphere; it is the side of caring, compassion and intuition (intuition, one should remember, simply means 'inner tuition'). Classically these are the characteristics that have been typically associated with the feminine.

THE MIND MIRROR

Male or female, *both* have left and right hemispheres. The differences between male and female attitudes is therefore predominantly due to a different balance between left and right hemisphere activity. Much of the work of the late Maxwell Cade was concerned with this area. He was interested in brain-rhythm activity and how it linked with meditational states. Geoff Blundell, of Audio Ltd, London, worked with Max to produce a spectrum analyser for the brain which is called the 'Mind Mirror'. This displays the activities of each side of the brain on an array of lights, the whole spectrum from the low-frequency delta waves, usually associated with deep sleep, right up to the wide-awake beta waves being displayed. The balance, or imbalance, between left and right brains can immediately be seen. A photograph of the latest Mind Mirror is shown in Figure 24, showing the details of the front panel.

What Max found was that men do indeed tend to use their left (logical) brains far more than their right brains. Many women predominantly use their right brains. However, the use of suitable meditation techniques can help to balance the activities of the two hemispheres, and Max also found that the more people worked on their own personal growth and went deeper into meditation, the more the two hemispheres balanced. Men who had shown little artistic talent found that they could do amazing artistic work, women who had been frightened of the intellect could hold their own in rational arguments. More than this, particular display patterns became evident on the Mind Mirror, these displays correlating closely with the mental state of the

138

Figure 24. The Mind Mirror machine for brain-wave analysis

subject, states such as 'State Five', sometimes called 'Cosmic Consciousness', which only appeared with skilled meditators or similarly adept people[22].

The dowsing information, wherever it may come from, first manifests within the right, non-logical, brain, for it is not a logical mind attribute, and hence the difficulty for someone who has an over-dominant left brain in accepting something like dowsing. In learning to dowse we are learning to unlock a latent ability of the intuitive mind. Unfortunately our whole western education system is geared to developing the logical mind. This can totally cripple personal growth, as creativity and compassion come from the other side of our natures. However, we do not have the

---

22. Cade, Maxwell C., and Coxhead, Nona, *The Awakened Mind*, Element Books, 1987.

monopoly of logical, male-type, dominance. Some cultures view the 'left side' of the body with disgust, calling it evil, while left handedness is looked upon as being devilish and an attribute to be stamped out as soon as possible.

A friend of mine once told me about the time that she taught a group of women from Pakistan. Their cultural roots were that of the Muslim faith. She told me how careful she had to be not to use her left hand for eating food or doing anything that could be done with the right hand alone, or this would have been taken as an insult by the other women. She said that her left side used to feel crippled by the time that she got home. Such things I have heard rationalised by the statement that in those countries it is the left hand that is used to clean the anus after going to the toilet. This I feel is just an attempt to justify something that goes much deeper. Those same cultures look upon left-handedness as something to be stamped out, they are very unhappy about the 'western' habit of allowing naturally left-handed children to write with their left hand.

If we also look at those same cultures we find that they are also male-dominated. Sexual equality is just not acceptable in a fundamentalist Muslim culture. If it is remembered that the left side of the body is connected to the right brain, then the reasons become clear: it is the feminine aspect that is being oppressed. The intuitive faculty is being treated as if it was evil It is noticeable that such societies are inevitably male dominated, women being looked down on as only existing to serve the dominant male. Such societies also show typical Rambo-like aggressive characteristics, as the quietening intuitive caring aspects of the female are being suppressed. The dominant logical male always feels threatened by the quiet intuitive female, because deep down it knows that the female is wiser than it is.

To those who do not like the above use of the words male and female I can only apologise. There really are no words to describe fully the aspects of the left and right brains without referring to everyday terminology. The Chinese concepts of Yang and Yin are really better perhaps, avoiding the more emotive aspects of the masculine and feminine principles.

So if we would become good or better dowsers one needs to befriend the right brain (left side) and learn to trust it. Taking an interest in art or music can help, and, some forms of meditation can be particularly inspiring. If ever someone says to you that dowsing is illogical and non-scientific, remember the split-brain experiments. We are much more than just a logical linear-time meat-machine!

CHAPTER 13

LEY LINES, BLACK STREAMS AND GEOPATHIC STRESS

The effects of the environment — including underground energy sources — are often not sufficiently acknowledged. Dowsing is applied in this area to reveal sources of stress, such as underground water flows, referred to as 'black streams'. These sources may affect both home and work environments, so dealing with them, in a manner determined by dowsing, can produce significant life-enhancing properties.

Over the centuries there have been folk takes about some places and houses being unhealthy to live in. In my part of Yorkshire such houses are often called 'Cancer Houses'. At one time, like many other people, I thought that such ideas were far-fetched, unless some obvious cause such as dampness was to blame. The idea that some sort of a curse could be on a building was too ridiculous for words.

Yet, there were houses where a succession of people had died from cancer and other stress-related illnesses. Houses where people, previously in good health, became ill shortly after moving into the house. I used to write such things off as coincidence, rather like the nuclear power industry's experts who have stated that leukaemia incidences near reprocessing plants must be coincidence, 'because there is no apparent reason for them to happen'. The risk is run of falling into the trap of saying that because no reason can be seen for it, it cannot happen.

In virtually all nations and cultures there is folk-lore about healthy and unhealthy places to live. In China there were the 'Dragonlines' which determined where houses should be built for the best health of their inhabitants. Fantasy? Or could there really be something in it?

Within the dowsing world there are acknowledged to be underground water flows that are commonly referred to as 'black streams'. These are underground streams that adversely affect the health of people and animals that live above them. I suspect that they were called 'black' from the traditional view that black is connected with the dark evil aspects of life. When using the Mager Rosette (see p. 50), if a reaction is obtained on the black sector, it is usually assumed that the water-flow has these health-destroying properties. The resulting stress on the human body is sometimes called 'water-stress', but this is not really an appropriate term, as the stress factor is not just owing to the water flow. The vast majority of underground water flows are perfectly benign.

A better expression is 'geopathic stress'. This is the term used in Germany, where there has been much interest and work done on the subject. Geopathic stress is a wider ranging term than that of black streams, covering any natural geological factor that causes health-threatening stress, and is thus an umbrella word that will cover all forms of earth-induced stress.

The last thing that I would like you to think is that such stress is common, and start panicking about it. Yes, it is relatively common, more so in some places than others, but not so common as some people make out. The warning signs are fairly clear. Illness occurs in otherwise previously healthy people, when they move house, even though there is no more obvious stress in their life than previously.

Moving house is always stressful, and it may take a little time to settle down into new surroundings. Yet when health is still poor after six months or so, with no obvious reason, then geopathic stress should be considered as a possibility. Some people always check a house for geopathic stress before moving in, this awareness being much more common in Germany and Austria than elsewhere.

The more obvious warning signs are a feeling of tension or coldness in some room or rooms of the house or place of work. Sometimes a feeling of dread will be experienced in going back to work or home although there may be much more down-to-earth reasons for this! In short there is a feeling of dis-ease even though there is no apparent reason for it. Stress-related illnesses such as cancer, MS, depression, inability to shake-off virus attacks, ME, etc., should all be taken as warnings to consider the possible occurrence of geopathic stress.

So what is geopathic stress, how is it caused, how can it be located, and what, if anything, can be done to neutralise it?

Geopathic stress is one of the areas, like dowsing, where one comes up against the fact that there is no explanation for its presence. There is plenty of evidence to show that it exists, but nothing concrete to give any indication of what it is. People use terms such as 'negative radiations' as if this explains what is going on, but basically nothing is known about what causes the effects. Radiation is just a convenient cover-up word.

The symptoms of geopathic stress are rather better known, and there are many things that have been known to cause the effect. Geological rockfaults, ley lines and black streams are common causes, even steel-frame buildings can cause it. In my part of the country, the most common cause is, without doubt, underground water flows.

In some areas, dissolved lead in underground water seems to be heavily implicated, and although the reason for this is not clear, the evidence is strong. Mrs Enid Smithett, past editor of the *BSD Journal*, told once how she traced a black stream over the fields on one of the Channel Islands. She was following the stream by dowsing and it was leading

144

towards the cliffs when a lady came out from one of the houses. When asked what she was doing, Enid told the lady how she was following a toxic underground water flow. 'Oh yes,' the lady said, 'we know about that. It comes out part-way down the cliffs where you were going. A child died last year from drinking the water.' It was Enid who then told me how she dealt with black stream by driving an iron rod into the ground directly over the stream on the upstream side of the house experiencing the trouble. This rod had the effect of neutralising the effect of the stream for a considerable distance downstream. She did not know how it worked, but assured me that it worked effectively. This is the basic method that I have now used successfully for many years, and I will give more details about treating these streams later on (see pp. 148–50).

At the 1976 Scottish congress of the BSD, David Steven, a Scottish shepherd from Dunnet, in the far north of Scotland, told about his experiences in this field[23]. He located a black stream by dowsing, and followed it down through Dunnet village until it flowed out under the sea. The stream followed the line of the road fairly closely as it bent through a right angle in the centre of the village, and it flowed under nearly all the houses at one side of the road. He then asked all the local people, many of whom had lived in the same houses for generations, how many people who had lived there had died of cancer. The map that he then produced was stunning, as nearly all the houses over the black stream had had cancer deaths, most with multiple deaths, some of them with five and six people dying. Nearly all the other houses were clear. The statistical chances of one side of a village street having many cancer deaths, the other side very few, are millions to one against this occurring.

It was this lecture that fired my own investigations into

23. Steven, David, 'Dowsing on a Scottish Farm', *BSD Journal*, December 1977, vol. 178.

geopathic stress. In the strange way that events seem to occur spontaneously on cue, it was only a few weeks later that I was asked if I could check on an Arts Centre not far away up the Yorkshire Dales. The two ladies who ran the place lived on the premises, which used to be a small country church. They had been so alarmed with the evil feelings in the place, that they had had the church exorcised by our local curate, who was a bit of a law unto himself and did it without asking for his bishop's permission.

After the exorcism the building felt considerably better, but it was not really right; the inhabitants were still unhappy about living there. My sister-in-law, Hilary, was in the curate's confidence so knew of what he had done. She mentioned my new interest in black streams and wondered if that could be the trouble. The upshot was that Hilary and I went off to see the building. I took with me a sledge-hammer and a miscellaneous collection of angle-iron lengths. I would have used rods, but I didn't have any suitable material to hand, and I couldn't see that the actual shape of the rod would matter.

I dowsed round the building with angle rods and the Mager Rosette. I found that I experienced two strong reactions, one stream just missing the building and the other cutting right under it just by the entrance porch. Never having tried my hand at such a thing before I dowsed for what length of iron I needed for each stream, and for the point to hammer the iron into the ground. Hilary was standing on the upstream side of one of the flows when I began hammering the angle-iron into the ground. 'What on earth are you doing?' she called to me, 'It feels terrible here.' Indeed it did. The downstream side of the rod dowsed quite clear as regards black on the rosette, but the upstream side felt strange. The experience I had was of being surrounded by swirling hostile energies.

This I had not expected. I was rather startled and worried. Upstream from the rod the stream flowed under the road which led up into the dales. I was concerned that someone sensitive could react to the effect when driving a car, and perhaps have an accident. I therefore went upstream from the road, into a car park, and put down an extra rod for each of the streams there. That seemed to do the trick. The road now felt perfectly OK.

Going inside the building, it felt better to both of us, but we realised that this could just be wishful thinking. However the two ladies reported back that after a week the place felt peaceful, and they were now happy to be living there.

There was an independent witness to the improvement. A friend of the ladies appeared about two months after our visit. He had not been there for about six months and knew nothing about what had been going on. 'What have you had done to the place?' he asked quite spontaneously. 'It feels much lighter. Have you had it redecorated or something?' In fact they had done nothing at all, the building was just the same as it had been previously.

The bottom line is that geopathic stress can seriously damage your health if nothing is done to remove its effects, but determining the presence of geopathic stress is, however, not easy unless you develop suitable dowsing skills. There are two electronic instruments made in Germany that can detect its presence. One of them, the 'Segmentograph', will be referred to a little later on (see p. 150). The other, the 'Vega' machine, can produce impressively accurate results by monitoring the electrical skin resistance at an acupuncture point. There is no doubt that this particular machine is operator-sensitive and has some similarities to the Black Box in that its circuits for testing samples against a patient have no obvious scientific basis. However this does not affect the accurate results that the machine can produce in skilled hands. The Vega machine has tests for the presence of geopathic stress on a patient, and I have been called out to see many houses to neutralise the stress that was revealed by the machine analysis. In every case so far I have found geopathic stress to be present when the Vega machine indicated its presence.

So how do we deal with such geopathic stress? What methods are used and how effective are they? Over the years, various people have used all sorts of techniques to remove the negative effects that result from people living or working in geopathically stressed places. The techniques vary enormously, crystals such as amethyst, coils of wire, baths of mineral oil, coloured card as well as metal stakes all being employed! All in all, this does not represent a collection of methods designed to instill confidence, yet there is no doubt that many of them can work.

The difficulty is that we are dealing with something intangible, even though its effects can be serious. The method that I now use is basically the same as previously mentioned, employing the use of metal rods driven into the ground. In addition I now always dowse for which metal to use, copper or iron, or even aluminium on rare occasions, and I dowse for what length of rod to use and where to hammer it in. I also dowse for whether more than one rod is needed, and quite often I find that two or even three rods are necessary to completely remove the effects. The diameter of the rod does not appear to be critical, and I often use 8-millimetre diameter rods of hard steel as these can be driven between paving stones if required.

My dowsing questions run as follows: whether I can deal with the problem satisfactorily; where to put the first rod; what material for the rod; and what length for the rod. Then after hammering the rod down to a depth where it will not be accidentally dug up (hopefully), I recheck to see if there is any negative effect still remaining. If so the process is repeated for a second, and occasionally third rod.

I had an excellent demonstration of the effectiveness of neutralising geopathic stress a few years ago. An orthodox medical consultant had bought a Vega machine and also the Segmentograph made by the same company. Neither machine would work when he tried them out. He contacted the manufacturers who asked him if he had had his consulting rooms checked for geopathic stress by a dowser. He said no

148

Figure 25. An electrical skin resistance meter (Audio Ltd.). Such instruments can help people to relax more completely, and thereby improve their dowsing skills.

and was sceptical about what they had told him. However he contacted the BSD who duly asked me if I could sort out his problem. I went to his house and found a black stream going directly under his consulting room, and this I duly

149

neutralised with two steel rods and then went back home. He rang me up a week later to say that after I had left, both machines had burst into life. He sent me Segmentograph traces of the same patient before and after my visit. In the first case the patient might just as well have been dead for all the response that was obtained! The Segmentograph works by subjecting segments of the body (hence its name) to small cyclical electric impulses, and notes the body's electrical activity that results from this stimulation. The bigger the change when the stimulation changes polarity or ceases, the more reactive that segment of the person's body is. Ideally the reactions should be moderate for all sections of the body. Too big a reaction shows an over-sensitivity to stress, too little shows a bodily (and often mental) withdrawal from the patient's personal circumstances. It is therefore quite scientific in its operation and does not depend on a skilled operator for its accuracy.

Something even more surprising happened about two years later. I received a 'phone call out of the blue — could I go down again as his machines had stopped working. The gardener had dug out the rods which the consultant had found in the hedge bottom. I arrived, put in some more rods, and the machines started to work again, a definite confirmation that the phenomenon is not all wishful thinking, as some people would have you believe.

So far I have been describing the effects of black streams. How about phenomena like rock faults and old mine shafts which are also suggested as being sources of geopathic stress? I employ exactly the same techniques when dealing with these, using rods, just as I do with black streams, and dowsing for where to put them in. In such cases it may take several rods spaced round a house to get the whole interior clear. It is not obvious why the method works in these cases, yet it appears to be entirely satisfactory in improving the health of people living above such areas.

There are other phenomena that create similar effects to black streams, such as ley lines and Curry and Hartmann grids.

There is much confusion and dissention in this area, and there seem to be as many ideas as there are enthusiasts pursuing the subject. The original concept of leys came from Alfred Watkins[24]. He noticed that there appeared to be long straight tracks connecting places of antiquity such as churches, dolmens and barrows. On the Ordnance Survey map, as many as five ancient sites could be found lying along the same straight line or track, within a significantly short distance and accurate to within one hundred feet or so. Watkins surmised that these alignments were deliberate and called them 'ley lines'. It was later that Guy Underwood[25] did some dowsing work and came up with the idea that there were also natural energy lines ('track lines', water lines' and 'aquastats') which he called 'geodetic lines'. Some of these were found along the straight (or ley) lines that linked ancient sites and the geodetic lines could be detected by the use of dowsing. Underwood also did much dowsing around the sites of antiquity themselves.

That was what started it all off. After about ten years 'ley hunting' got under way. The renewed modern interest in ancient sites catalysed the whole thing and many eager-beavers started dowsing for ley lines, sometimes I suspect with little idea what they were dowsing for. It was also of note that not everyone came up with the same energy patterns as Guy Underwood had done, indeed the majority of people achieved quite different results. This difference between the results of 'energy fields' dowsed by different people is a factor that turns up time and time again. I would like to repeat my warnings of not being carried away by wishful thinking. It is all to easy, in such a nebulous area, to dowse and find the products of expectation or imagination, rather than what is really there. Also when dowsing for

---

24. Watkins, Alfred, *The Old Straight Track*, Methuen, 1925.

25. Underwood, Guy, *The Pattern of the Past*, Museum Press, 1968.

something that is, after all, pretty intangible, it is easy to phrase one's dowsing question incorrectly or for it to be too broad in concept.

So just what are these ley lines? My own dowsing would suggest that there are several different categories of them, although their effects may be similar.

Firstly, there seem to be straight energy lines that one can detect by dowsing, these lines affecting the health of people adversely. These lines do not appear to be linked with obvious alignments through churches and ancient monuments. In the absence of any other information, it can be assummed that these are natural energy forces associated with the earth.

Next, there are straight energy lines that *do* align with churches, ancient monuments, etc. Usually these do not affect people adversely — in fact to the contrary, they can have healing effects. One should beware however, it is not necessarily wise to live on such a line, one can have too much of a good thing. These lines are probably natural, ancient people having deliberately sited their places of worship on them, their preference being for a point where two or more such lines crossed.

Finally, there are those lines that are man-made. Sometimes these appear spontaneously where there is serious illness at a site which was previously clear. Sometimes these lines are made by acts of ritual or other mind-concentrating methods. In other words, it appears that energy lines can be created (or rather activated) by conscious or unconscious action.

One can attempt to classify lines, dowsing then being used to categorise the types of line, but this will not be conclusive. One may be simply dowsing for what one's conscious mind believes. Ultimately, all one can do is steadily and carefully gather factual information and look for patterns in that information.

Be that as it may, it remains a fact that many people have taken to ley hunting both by looking for alignments on maps and also by dowsing for ley lines. To many people it has become a fascinating and valuable interest, and their researches will bare fruit for future generations.

Out of this dowsing for ley lines has come a welter of information, much of which is suspect. According to some people the whole earth is covered with grids of energy lines. One of these, the Hartmann Grid[26] has lines spaced only a matter of two metres apart. A whole mystical industry seems to be building up around these things, and many of the theories are based more on wishful thinking than on firm evidence. Certainly such grids of lines do not turn up in my dowsing when looking for geopathic stress. This is not to say that practitioners who neutralise such systems are charlatans and frauds, no — things are not that simple. The person who clears geopathic stress, discovered by dowsing, may be in reality acting more as a healer than anything else. In other words, when is geopathic stress, geopathic stress? Certainly the amount of geopathic stress discovered from Vega tests is not as high as would be expected from a consideration of the Hartmann (2 × 2.5 metres) and Curry (22 metres square) grids.

As an example of how difficult a matter we are dealing with, consider the Christmas Edition of *Tomorrow's World* of several years ago. A machine was demonstrated that, according to its inventor, would produce ley lines that dowsers could locate. At first sight the results that they showed looked quite impressive. If the machine was switched on, dowsers gave a positive reaction when crossing its beam, even though they did not know whether it was on or off. Likewise when it was off they showed no reaction, and this appeared to prove that the machine worked. There was however a problem, the inventor was switching it on or off, so someone knew whether the machine was in its on or off state. I described earlier (see p. 55) how my dowsing could

---

26. Morley, Anthony Scott, *Journal of Alternative Medicine*, May 1985.

be influenced by what my sister-in-law was thinking, and this is the fatal flaw in all such tests.

There should have been a random internal switch in the machine, so that no-one knew whether it was on or off until after the dowsing had taken place. Also the construction of the machine was suspect. It used a quartz–halogen car headlamp bulb as its source. Now sunlight radiates all the frequencies that are covered by such light bulbs, so in sunlight we should have immensely strong ley lines reflecting all over the place! What the experiment did prove was that dowsers could be influenced by the thoughts or expectations of others. Certainly careful tests to achieve positive results with such equipment with double-blind tests have failed.

Wishful thinking and being open to the influence of others can easily wreck dowsing results and make them meaningless. This is not to say that natural energy lines do not exist, but simply to point out that one has to take the extravagant claims of some people with a large pinch of salt.

From my experience, ley lines, or whatever else you care to call them, do certainly exist, but not in vast numbers. I find that black streams and earth faults contribute far more to cases of ill health, particularly the former. My basis for saying this is quite simple. If something runs in a dead straight line then it is highly unlikely to be an underground water flow, except for flows in old mine workings. The vast majority of negative influence lines that I find causing health problems do not go in straight lines, but follow a varying path. When the negative effect has been neutralised, then usually I find a reaction on the Mager Rosette corresponding to water purity. One can also depth the flow with no problem.

When I have come across what I term a ley line — a straight line influence that seems to run on indefinitely — then inevitably it has had a serious effect on the health of those living within its influence. Also the effect is not so easy to neutralise. I remember one beautiful cottage in

154

Lancashire that I was called out to look at. It looked idyllic, but you could have cut the heavy atmosphere with a knife. The lady living there was having severe health problems, and indications of geopathic stress had come up strongly on the Vega machine. I found a dead straight line travelling about south to north through the house. It took three rods to clear the effect, one aluminium, one copper and one iron, all of different lengths. I dowsed for which metal to use first, then the position to put the rod in, and finally what length to use. I repeated this until I obtained a 'yes' to the question, 'Have I now neutralised the adverse effects on people living in the house?'

Why the three metals? The answer is that I just don't know. At the moment we are really in the information gathering stage, and until sufficient information has been gathered in any investigation, then theorising will not only be premature but can give rise to incorrect ideas that can impede final understanding.

The lady who lived in the cottage being affected by the ley line made a remarkable recovery. In the words of the practitioner who did the Vega analysis, 'She is now dancing around like a spring chicken!'

Sometimes it may be impractical to treat a building. I was asked by a schoolmaster about treating the main school building where he worked. 'Only if I get permission from the Head,' I answered. There was no way I would go sticking rods in the ground of the school without permission! I said that I could do a map dowse if he sent me an accurate scale plan, then *he* could put the rods in. He never wrote back to me. Sometimes it is easy to become involved with someone else's problem at a level where it is you, not them, who will catch any flack that is flying around.

Geopathic stress can extend for quite a few metres each side of the centre line of the black stream, ley line, etc. It is therefore not correct that just moving a bed a few centimetres, for example, will remove the influence. I think that this idea arises from the Hartmann grid concept where the

155

grid lines are said to be usually about 20 cm wide. This is not my experience. Checking carefully for toxic effects, my dowsing indicates that they normally fall off quite slowly from each side of the main influence line. I find that one needs to be about 3 metres to the side of the line of influence to be sure that the effects will not be noticeable. The effects will be worst if you are smack over the centre, so any move away will be of benefit.

Again, check it out for yourself. You may find that I am completely wrong, and that Hartmann and/or Curry grids do exist. I mentioned earlier how easy it is to be swayed by other people's ideas and concepts. I *think* that I have been completely objective in my work on earth energies, but one must always leave room to change one's ideas. No-one is infallible.

Geopathic stress at a place of work can be quite a problem. If you have this then there are several possible courses of action. If the management agree, then neutralisation is by far the best cure. Failing this, try to see if it is possible to move your desk or the place you usually work. If this is not possible, then you are in the region of needing some other method of clearing your working space.

There have been many devices put on the market for clearing geopathic stress in small areas. Some of them are expensive for what they are. They seem to be based on a wide variety of principles, some use crystals, some use metals, some use alternating metal and organic materials, like Reich's Orgone Accumulator[27]. Perhaps the cheapest, and one of the most effective methods, is to obtain a cluster of amethyst crystals and place it just by where you work. Take it home about once a fortnight and give it a good wash in clear water to 'recharge' it. It may sound totally crazy, but more often than not this works well. I have also used large

---

27. Reich, Wilhelm, *The Orgone Energy Accumulator*, Orgone Institute Press, Rangeley, Maine, 1951.

fluorite crystals mounted with their axis vertical to good effect.

It is even possible to neutralise effects by working on maps. I first heard about this method of neutralisation from Enid Smithett. She works extensively from maps to dowse for black streams and other sources of geopathic stress. One day, someone had sent her a map for analysis. The person rang up in the evening to see what Enid had found. She took the map and dowsed over it whilst talking to the person on the telephone. She was using a pin as a pointer, and when the pendulum indicated the correct spot for treatment on the site, she stuck the pin into the map to mark the correct place. 'What have you done?' asked the lady at the other end of the 'phone, 'The house suddenly feels a lot lighter!' On checking the house on the plan with dowsing, it was found that the pin in the map had neutralised the black stream! I would not like to give the idea that this method is as good as working on the site, usually this is not the case. Nevertheless when it is difficult to get to a particular place, working on a map may be a considerable help even if not providing a complete cure.

One lady who went on one of my courses asked for help, but the only problem was that she lived in Windsor and I was not going anywhere near there in the foreseeable future. I said that I would try working from a map, which she then sent to me. I found a *band* of stress that cut right through her house, something I have not experienced since. It was about 4 metres wide and went straight through the living room and bedroom. I dowsed for the places where rods should be driven into the ground, and marked those places with a small cross surrounded by a circle. I think that I found five that were needed to clear the effects from the house. I then checked the house on the map, and to my surprise it now gave no reaction to geopathic stress. I had been expecting to put five pins in the map, but they seemed not to be needed.

The lady rang me up about a week later. Both she and her

husband, who was a complete sceptic, were much better in health and they stayed that way for a few years. She then contacted me and said that their health was suffering again. I rechecked the map and found that the situation had altered. I rubbed out the old pencil marks and started again. The band of stress had changed direction and width, and needed different treatment points to the previous time. Again I was contacted about a week later and told that their health was back to normal.

For those wishing to try dowsing for geopathic stress I would counsel caution. It is easy to become carried away with fanciful ideas and find problems all over the place. Equally you may miss a source of stress and still have problems that have not been dealt with. It is a field that is best left until you have developed a good dowsing accuracy in some other area, after all we are dealing with a pretty intangible phenomenon, and to be safe one needs to have both feet planted firmly on the ground before starting.

CHAPTER 14

OTHER APPLICATIONS TO HEALING

Dowsing can be successfully applied in the healing fields of aromatherapy, acupuncture, spinal adjustment (for the expert only), and medical herbalism. The author describes his work in these areas and pin-points the problems as well as the advantages. The approach in all cases is a holistic one, considering all aspects of the person's welfare, encouraging the immune system to develop its strength.

This chapter is about other uses of dowsing, some of which need special skills and therefore should not be entered into without suitable training.

As it will now be appreciated, dowsing can be used for a variety of diagnostic and treatment purposes within the healing field. Indeed it is difficult to envisage an area where it does not have an application. Take, for instance, aromatherapy, the ancient treatment of illness with the aromatic essential oils from plants. Aromatherapy has taken a steadily increasing importance within the complementary healing field, often being allied with massage techniques. There is a long list of possible essential oils that are available, all of which are well documented as to their therapeutic effects. There is however a problem in that what do you use when someone comes to you with a symptom that is not covered by the information that you have on the oils? What do you do when there are several possible oils? Do you use just one or the lot? How do you choose?

In such areas dowsing can be helpful. It is also well worth remembering that dowsing can give you an insight into the patient that might otherwise be missed. If you dowse for which essential oil(s) should be used with a particular patient, then the results may mean that you treat perhaps less obvious yet more important facets of that person's make up. It is too easy to go for the obvious. For instance, suppose that someone is just feeling run down and asks for a relaxing aromatherapy massage. This would perhaps suggest using camomile, or neroli, or similar oils. However, suppose dowsing brought up sage and rosemary oils. This would suggest that the cause of that run-down feeling needs treating. There are strong indications with the latter oils that the person was feeling run-down owing to a sluggish lymph system. In this case a lymph drainage massage could be helpful, perhaps accompanied by counselling about what could be causing the trouble (diet, etc.). An experienced aromatherapist would probably spot what was needed, but in addition dowsing can be a helpful tool in gaining insight into a patient's condition and selecting the most appropriate and effective method of treatment.

Dowsing can be used with acupuncture. I realise that purists may well throw up their hands in horror at the thought, feeling that classical diagnosis is all that is needed. Dare I say it again, but feeling that one must always slavishly follow the 'correct' way of working will inevitably stifle one's own creative ability and also often result in one being of less benefit to the patient. After all it is the patient that matters in the end.

For a period I used to cooperate with an acupuncturist who worked in Derbyshire. She was skilled, but found that some patients just did not respond to treatment. She was doing everything by the book but nothing happened to these patients. She met me on a weekend course that I was running, and asked me if I could dowse for her patients over the telephone. I warned her that I had only a basic knowledge of acupuncture, but said that so long as she took responsibility for checking my results, I would have a go.

What followed was fascinating. She would ring me up about a patient and tell me their symptoms. Perhaps treatment on the lung meridian was positively indicated but she was obtaining no response when stimulating the correct points. She would call out the numbers of the meridian points one at a time over the telephone and I would tell her when I experienced a positive dowsing response from my pendulum. The numbers meant nothing to me, I had no idea of the properties of any of the points. The points that I selected were always different from those that she had been using and quite often were points that, although known of, little was known about. Nearly always her unresponsive patients responded to the treatment of these new points that had been determined by dowsing.

I use dowsing frequently in my spinal adjustment work. This is definitely an area to be approached with great caution and one *must* be adequately trained before using any force on another person's spine, *particularly if they may be suffering from osteoporosis.* With adequate basic training, dowsing can then be a great help in any manipulation work. For a start, one can dowse down the spine to see which areas have nerves that are under pressure. This can cause a great variety of symptoms that may not seem to be related to the spine at all.

A colleague at Bradford University who came to see me once was suffering from swelling in one foot. He had heard of my work and was obviously pretty dubious about it all. The foot problem had been diagnosed as bursitis; he had had it for about ten weeks and it was getting no better. He had been given cortisone injections, which had not helped, and was told that all being well the swelling would go away on its own. No time scale was given for its possible departure.

I checked over the foot with my pendulum, but could find nothing that was the cause of the problem. I then checked up the leg and into the spine, my question being, 'Where

161

can I best treat this condition?' I experienced a strong reaction in the lower thoracic spine, — much to my surprise. That was the only place I could find any reaction. I then asked the question, 'Is it correct to give treatment at this point?' The answer was 'yes'. By a series of questions and answers I determined that there was a nerve trapped at that point and that a rotation of the spine was needed to free it. I got him down on my office floor (after getting his permission!), and gave his spine an adjustment *in the direction determined by my dowsing*. It is worth noting here that by dowsing it is possible to obtain information about how to carry out manipulative treatment.

He got up after the treatment, thanked me and hobbled away. A week later he came back to see me. His foot was by then nearly fully recovered, but please could I have a look to see if any further treatment was needed? It was, but my dowsing indicated that nothing more would be needed after that final treatment.

Two weeks later it was the staff Easter walk over the Lakeland Fells, this being about 20 kilometres or so in length. My patient was there with no foot problems at all. I felt that it was grossly unfair that he finished up in considerably better shape than I did at the end of the walk!

It was about a year later that the probable explanation emerged of the need for spinal manipulation at the point found by dowsing. I was running a weekend course on dowsing, and gave a demonstration of the use of the pendulum in manipulative therapy. I mentioned my experience when treating the bursitis the previous year. There was an acupuncturist present on the course who was interested in the case. He queried exactly where the pain and swelling were present in the foot, also just where I had manipulated the spine. It turned out that the pain in the foot could well have come from what the acupuncturists call the Alarm Point for the kidneys. That particular area can become tender and inflamed if there is impaired kidney function. The point on the back that I had manipulated was just above the line of the kidneys, so it could well have been affecting kidney function.

Unfortunately even within complementary medicine there is too much specialisation of knowledge. This means that information does not become cross-fertilised between the different methods of working to anything like the degree that it could. In particular, osteopathy, chiropractic, acupuncture and shiatsu have much in common. Orthodox medicine is often criticised for being too specialised, forgetting that the unorthodox can be just as isolationist and elitist in its own way, if not more so at times.

Pressure on nerves in the spine can cause a range of problems that orthodox medicine can do little to treat, orthodox medicine, that is, so far as the UK is concerned. I still find it incredible that osteopathy and chiropractic are not accepted within the orthodox field in this country. Perhaps it is because the claims of those professions seem too great for the orthodox medics to accept. As in the case of my colleague, how could pressure on a nerve in the spine cause bursitis in the foot? This is another example of being trapped into feeling that unless what is observed can be explained within existing theories, then that phenomenon is suspect. Like dowsing!

After a television appearance by Major Bruce McManaway, he was flooded with enquiries for healing sessions with him. To help cope with the flood, I saw quite a few people from the north of England. One Saturday afternoon a man, accompanied by his wife, came to see me. I thought that he looked a bit puzzled when I invited them in. I sat them down and then asked him what the problem was.

He was disturbed and quite angry. 'I thought that we were just going out for a run in the country,' he said, 'I had no idea that my wife had booked me in to see you. Who are you anyway? What are your qualifications, and how do you work?' Looking back I am surprised that I didn't just tear a long strip off his wife for booking in her husband under false pretences, and send them away. However as I was not pressed for time I spent the next twenty minutes talking about how I worked.

The man then looked up at me abruptly. 'If you are any good,' he said, 'you will be able to tell me what the matter is with me. I went to the doctor yesterday and he gave me a full examination.'

To say I was floored was putting it mildly. I was angry at being put in such a position, on trial as it were, and I wonder why I didn't just tell him to b*** off!

However I didn't. I checked carefully down his spine and found severe pressure on nerves in the lower neck. I told him of my findings. 'What symptoms could that cause?' he asked. 'In that area, most likely pain in the right shoulder which could well travel down the right arm, even as far as the hand,' I replied.

His face softened for the first time since I had met him. 'You may be interested to know that I went to my doctor with a pain in my neck which went down into my right arm,' he said. 'The doctor told me that it was most likely caused by a trapped nerve in the neck, and that he could do nothing for it!'

Needless to say he then allowed me to work on his neck, freeing the trap on the nerve and relieving the pain.

I am still surprised that under such extreme provocation my dowsing skills held up. Perhaps it was because I was angry and felt that I had nothing to loose. Certainly I do not recommend doing one's dowsing under such difficult conditions.

In my part of the world there is a great shortage of skilled medical herbalists. Considering that the vast majority of our modern drugs have their origins in herbs, it is surprisingly difficult to find people who still practise with the natural substance. It is always worth bearing in mind that the natural substance can have different, and often gentler, effects than the synthetic product.

I once talked about this to a neighbour, who was a pharmacist. He told me that usually the natural product was better. The problem with natural drugs was that their potency varied from year to year and place to place. Synthetics were accurately reproducible. Also it was possible to patent the synthetic drugs and therefore make large profits. No-one made much profit from natural drugs as there was open competition and anyone could make them. So basically there were two factors that tended to favour synthetic drugs, and as usual the strongest one was making more money (I am not criticising the drug companies as such when I say this, but pointing out a fact of human nature).

My experience is that natural products do not appear to have such violent side-effects as synthetic drugs. My neighbour confirmed this. 'Take the case of Aspirin,' he said. 'The synthetic drug is a pure single chemical, acetylsalicylic acid. The original extract from Willow Bark contained not one, but a whole series of related salicylates, the net effect of which was to give a less harsh action on the body.'

As an example, take the traditional use of raspberry leaf tea for an easy childbirth. A typical old-wives tale some people may say. Not so. One research lecturer at Bradford University examined the constituents of raspberry leaf tea and found in it chemicals similar to ergot, but of gentler action. Ergot, you may know, is produced by mouldy grain and can cause abortion in pregnant women. These related compounds in the raspberry leaf cause the muscles of the uterus to expand and contract and so strengthen them, thus leading to an easy childbirth when the correct time arrives.

In the absence of a local medical herbalist, it is possible to dowse for which herb will be beneficial. I have done this successfully and on one occasion pennyroyal was indicated when dowsing for a friend of mine. I went into Robinsons of Bradford, the dispensing herbalists, and asked if they stocked it. The old man behind the counter gave me a strange look. 'I will just see if I have to open a new sack for you!' he said, as he went off into the back of the shop with a twinkle in his eye. I didn't know that it is one of the most common herbs used in herbal medicine. As before, *it is*

165

essential to check all dowsing results with a good textbook on the subject to make sure that the remedy and dose have no contra-indications for the patient that you are prescribing for. In dealing with something as intangible as dowsing it must always be remembered that mistakes can be made, even by the most experienced person. Once you believe that your dowsing is infallible, you are setting yourself up for what could be a very hard lesson!

CHAPTER 15

IMPLICATIONS FOR HEALING

Health and healing are becoming consumer-led revolutions, and what was unacceptable yesterday is today's force for change, development and growth. Dowsing belongs in this process as its effectiveness and its possibilities are realised. Dowsing is a gateway into expanded areas of consciousness, and within such expansion there is always personal growth.

It appears that people have always tried to find explanations for illnesses and plagues. It has been an area full of superstition and false beliefs. The law on blasphemy was brought into being because it was thought that anyone who cursed God, or made mockery of Him, brought retribution on the whole population, not just the perpetrator. Under such circumstances of belief, such a law to protect the general population made sense. (Also it is a convenient device to explain plagues, etc., and the local heretic then makes a suitable scapegoat!)

Then the modern period of scientific enlightenment came. Illness was caused by microbes of varying sorts: nothing mystical, just a simple scientific explanation. The work of Pasteur seemed to prove beyond all doubt that bacteria (and later viruses) were responsible. Yet no-one seemed to notice what Pasteur said on his death-bed. Translated it meant, 'I got it all wrong, the microbe it is nothing, its environment is everything!' What he had realised was that not everyone contracted illnesses in times of plague. Therefore it was the

167

differences between people that mattered. In other words, why was it that some people became ill, even died, and others remained perfectly well?

Modern research has uncovered much information about the body's auto-immune system and how it fights off illness, yet still too often we are looking in the wrong direction. We look for higher and higher powered drugs, spend vast sums on medical research, often for little result, yet far too often we do not look carefully at the patients themselves: the 'environment' of the illness.

To understand why medical research has taken the direction it has, we only need to look at the environment in which the research takes place and decisions are made. My background is that of the university system, I know it well!

The common fallacy about universities is that they are places where dedicated individuals work in their Ivory Towers pushing back the frontiers of knowledge, their only interest being scientific truth (even if it may be rather useless at times). Not so. University lecturers and professors are human like everyone else. There is jealousy, in-fighting and political gerrymandering of the highest order. Indeed, because colleges are relatively enclosed institutions, this makes it all the worse. Promotion is usually dependent on having sufficient research papers published in refereed journals. For research to be accepted as being original, this generally means that it needs to be somewhat abstruse. I read where someone did a survey of papers published by the Institute of Mathematics. The results of that survey indicated that on average each paper published was read *and thoroughly understood* by an average of 0.6 of a person! So one third of all the papers were never really understood by anyone apart from the writer (or they were not interested in trying to understand them).

The first classic university problem is finding original research topics. There is much that we need to know. There are yawning gaps in our knowledge about many things so what is the problem? Usually it is that these areas of need

168

are not original enough, they are too 'obvious'. The fact that the information is needed and not known is irrelevant; they are not sufficiently academically challenging.

The second problem is that of finance. From where can staff receive financial support for research students and allied support staff? Bodies like the Medical Research Council and the Scientific Research Council, which are government funded, have an extensive old-boy network which tends to maintain the status quo. Otherwise in areas of health and medicine nearly all the money will inevitably come from the drug companies with their strong interest in new drugs.

What is needed is more support for what is called 'clinical ecology', in other words the personal environmental factors that contribute to illness. This has some support in the USA, but in the UK clinical ecologists tend to be looked down on by the established medical practitioners. 'It's not the real medicine — they are just playing about,' was one comment I heard.

There have been lone voices in the wilderness, Prof. Birkett with his work on dietary fibre for one. It took about twenty years before his results became acceptable to orthodoxy. Prof. Yudkin's work on sugar[28] is still meeting violent opposition from vested interests, even though the case against sugar, except in *small* quantities is inescapable. If sugar consumption was drastically reduced, particularly in children, then the controversial fluoridation of water would be unnecessary. Enough is already known, yet nothing happens!

Prof. Linus Pauling in the USA, with Dr Cameron of Scotland, showed that vitamin C has anti-cancer properties, yet this is not a recognised part of cancer treatment. Vitamin C is, of course, non-proprietary and very cheap. Again, no interest showed in following up the work.

When one understands the ecology of medical research,

---

28. Yudkin, John, *Pure White and Deadly*, Viking, 1986.

then the reasons for the absence of research into fields of vital importance becomes obvious: possible promotion, acceptability and money lie elsewhere. Human nature again.

Health and healing, like environmental concern, are becoming consumer-led revolutions. For too long our Ministries of the Environment, Agriculture and Health have been concerned with the producers, not the consumers. Indeed, sceptics have said that they are really concerned with the opposite, destroying the environment, destroying agricultural land, and being concerned with illness. Changes have for too long been decided by consultation with those who control how the money is spent, not with those who have the money spent on them.

I remember listening to a programme, years ago, on the radio, when consumers were just waking up to the possible benefits of wholemeal bread. An expert dietitian, I believe from the Ministry of Agriculture, categorically stated that it was a complete fallacy. 'White bread is just as nutritious as wholemeal. It is just a group of food cranks who are irresponsibly attacking perfectly wholesome food,' she replied. So much for experts!

It is small wonder that the average consumer is becoming more and more skeptical about the quality of the information that they are fed from official sources. As someone once said, 'I am fed up with being treated like a mushroom. Kept in the dark and fed on s***!'

We should not therefore be unduly surprised that little genuine research has been done by official sources into complementary methods of healing. There is little to motivate the researchers in those directions. The attitude of my colleagues at Bradford University when I was doing my first investigations into dowsing ranged from interest (in just a few people) to definite hostility. I remember one member of staff telling me he thought that my investigations brought the college into disrepute. If he had had the power I am sure that he would have had my investigations censured and stopped immediately.

170

Such bigotism appears even when you try to keep things clearly in the scientific area with only tenuous connections into the unknown. One year I suggested a final-year project topic of looking into the electrical responses in plants. From an electronics point of view it was a reasonable topic, as it posed interesting difficulties in detecting the information present in a growing plant without picking up spurious signals. In the description to the project I pointed out the work done by Cleve Backster[29] in the USA and how people had criticised his techniques.

The student that took on the project was not one of the best that I supervised. Unfortunately he was full of ideas and talk, but of little practical ability. His work dragged on and on. Finally I virtually had to show him how to do it. His results were poor and decidedly inadequate in quality for a final-year degree student. At the examiner's meeting I was astounded at the attitude of the external examiner and some of my colleagues. The project that I had suggested, not the student's inadequate performance, was criticised! 'A very unsuitable project,' the external examiner called it.

Emotion had totally clouded the issue. The basis of the project was finding how to obtain accurate measurements from living plants *irrespective of the information obtained from those measurements and the possible interpretations of that information.* After all, information is just that, information. I was not expecting the student to make any earth-shattering measurements, just to see what signals, if any, could be obtained with 100 per cent confidence that they were real, not artifacts. Even the possible presence of such electrical signals was sufficient to cause an immense amount of hostility. So much for having an open scientific mind.

There are some universities and colleges that are now beginning to investigate such areas of the unknown, but it takes a pretty determined research worker to make any

29. Watson, Lyall, *Supernature*, pp. 247–9, Hodder and Stoughton, 1973.

progress. After all, where will one publish such work? The journal *Nature*, for example seems to have totally compromised what should be a forum for work honestly carried out.

So why should there be such hostility to subjects like dowsing and complementary medicine? I suspect the same reasons that heretics used to be burned at the stake and modern fundamentalists seem to burn with so much hate. Quite simply — fear.

When we are really sure of ourselves, when we *know* things from our own experience, rather than just having been indoctrinated into believing them, then we have no fear. A defensive, and therefore aggressive, attitude always indicates that a person is fearful, has something to hide, and hence the futility of trying to convince people, by argument, of the reality of such phenomena as dowsing. If people believe that such things cannot exist then they will feel threatened by the suggestion that they do. Indeed people will do anything to protect their beliefs: lie, cheat, murder — no limits!

Politics and religion, those twin areas of dedicated beliefs, have caused the vast majority of all wars and serious conflicts in the world. Some religions condemn dowsing as being the work of the Devil!

True religion has nothing to fear from anything. The word religion comes from the Latin *Re Ligere* which means, if my Latin is correct, to rejoin — to become one again. Religion should therefore only be concerned with the quest to become reunited with the supreme creative force. It is the power politics and elitism of religions that belie their name and show their actual purpose.

Dowsing is a gateway into expanded areas of consciousness. Within such expansion there is always personal growth. Experiencing more and more of the reality of existence cannot but broaden one's vision, providing that there is good will and openness.

Providing that one keeps one's feet firmly on the ground,

172

dowsing is absolutely safe. Providing that flights of fantasy are not allowed to take over, dowsing can be an invaluable skill in helping us to live our lives with more skill. These are the reasons why I always suggest using dowsing for the ordinary, everyday things of life, like diet and improving health. If other things develop, such as interest in such things as personal growth, meditation, spirituality — fine. The main point is that such interest should not be forced. I have seen too many people try to use religion as an escape from the world, rather than use this world as a stepping stone into greater areas of awareness.

Dowsing is therefore a bridge between the logical mind and the intuitive mind. We need to build these bridges. The logical mind without the inspiration of the intuitive is sterile and has no compassion or feeling. Wars are hatched and run by people with such lack of intuitive guidance, who see things in terms of black and white, good and evil.

It is time for the feminine intuitive aspect in man and woman to take its rightful place, at the head of the table. The intuitive should be supported by the logical, not vice versa. We must allow the dowsing to tell us how things are *and not allow the logical mind to interfere*. The logical mind is fine for carrying things out and questioning if things appear to be stupid or dangerous, but in the final event we have to learn to trust the intuitive aspects of our natures. Only this way will we become more loving, more at ease, and fully skilled in the world.

There is a saying, 'As above, so below.' Equally we could say, 'As within, so without.' What we feel inside reflects out into the world. If we are unbalanced within, this will reflect out into imbalance in the way that we deal with the world and other people. If the intuitive side is largely ignored then the masculine side will over-dominate and show as aggression towards others. This is the message that the world has for us at this present moment: in far too many people the feminine side is mistrusted and suppressed. I am supporting balance in both men and women, the balance where

173

male and female live in harmony within and without.

Pie in the sky? Perhaps for the world — who knows? Yet it is not impossible for the one being that we do have total charge over, namely ourselves.

Dowsing has revolutionised my life. It started me on a path from which I am happier than I ever dreamed possible. The ache in my heart has gone, there is now a lightness in my step. Dowsing has helped to heal me in a way that I never expected, bringing me more and more into a unity.

There is an ancient Chinese saying, 'The longest journey begins with the first step.' Often that first step into the longest journey, that of self-discovery, can be difficult. My first step was trying out dowsing. Perhaps it might be yours as well.

APPENDIX 1

USEFUL ADDRESSES *

HOMEOPATHIC EDUCATIONAL SERVICES, 2124N Kittredge, Berkeley, California 94704. Offers a free catalog of books, tapes and medicines. (Please send a self-addressed, stamped envelope.)

INSTITUTE OF HEALTH SCIENCES, 975E Hornblend, San Diego, California 92109. Write for a free brochure.

RADIONICS INSTITUTE, 411N-75 Eastdale, Toronto, Canada M4C 5N3. Offers correspondence courses, certification and equipment.

BODY THERAPY INSTITUTE, P.O. Box 202, Saxapahaw, North Carolina 27340. Offers certification programs and continuing education seminars.

LIFE UNDERSTANDING FOUNDATION, Box 729A, Stanwood, Washington 98292. Write for a complete catalog of dowsing implements, instructional videotapes and books.

THE DENALI CENTER FOR HOLISTIC HEALTH AND PERSONAL GROWTH, Hwy. C. 89, Box 451, Willow, Alaska 99688-9705. Offers a wide variety of divination and healing services. (Please send self-addressed, stamped envelope.)

THE ASSOCIATION FOR RESEARCH AND ENLIGHTENMENT, P.O. Box 595, Virginia Beach, Virginia 23451. The ARE is a firmly established alternative center.

THE HEALTHVIEW NEWSLETTER, 612 Rio Road West, Box 6670, Charlottesville, Virginia 22906. A periodical publication supported by a number of natural-healing oriented physicians, dentists and chiropractors. Provides additional information about alternative medical treatments.

---

*This list is merely a guideline for obtaining additional information. The publisher has no knowledge of the purported existence of these organizations or the quality of their services.

APPENDIX 2

RECOMMENDED DAILY ALLOWANCES OF MINERALS AND VITAMINS

(Milligrams unless otherwise stated)

MINERALS	UK		USA	
	Adults	Pregnant Women	Adults	Pregnant Women
Calcium	500	1200	800	1200
Chloride	None	None	3400	3400
Chromium*	None	None	125	125
Copper	None	None	2.5	2.5
Iodine*	140	140	150	150
Iron	12	15	18	48
Magnesium	None	None	350	450
Phosphorus	None	None	800	1200
Potassium	None	None	3750	3750
Selenium*	None	None	125	125
Sodium	None	None	2200	2200
Zinc	None	None	15	20

* *Micrograms*

VITAMINS	UK		USA	
	Men	Women	Men	Women
Vitamin A*	750	750	800	1000
Thiamine	1.1	0.9	1.4	1.0
Riboflavin	1.7	1.3	1.6	1.2
Niacin	18	15	20	18
Pyridoxine	None	None	2.0	2.0
Vitamin B12*	None	None	3.0	3.0
Vitamin C	30	30	45	45
Vitamin D*	2.5	2.5	7	5
Vitamin E	None	None	15	12
Folic Acid	300	300	400	400

* *Micrograms*

INDEX